Euthanasia – Choice and Death

Books in the Series

Published

New Terror/New Wars
Paul Gilbert

Forthcoming

First World/Third World
Michael Edwards

Should We Give to Aid Agencies?
Keith Horton

Euthanasia – Choice and Death

Gail Tulloch

Edinburgh University Press

© Gail Tulloch, 2005

Edinburgh University Press Ltd
22 George Square, Edinburgh

Typset in Sabon
by TechBooks, and
printed and bound in Great Britain
by MPG Books Ltd, Bodmin

A CIP record for this book is available
from the British Library

ISBN 0 7486 2247 0 (hardback)
ISBN 0 7486 1881 3 (paperback)

The right of Gail Tulloch
to be identified as author of this work
has been asserted in accordance with
the Copyright, Designs and Patents Act 1988.

In memory of my parents
Pat and Bon
And with love to my children
Andy and Deb
and their children
Lachie and Mia

Contents

Series Preface   ix
Acknowledgements   xiii

Part One

1   Choice and Death   3
    Biological death   4
    Human death   4
    The good death   6
    Defining death   7
    The Harvard definition of brain death   9
    The brain   12
    Defining death: selective non-treatment of severely
       disabled newborns   14

2   Stark Choices   23
    Conceptual distinctions   24
    The slippery slope   32
    Voluntary/involuntary, active/passive euthanasia   33
    For and against euthanasia   34
    Resource allocation choices   37
    Two examples of decision procedures   39
    The individual and the state   41
    The man on the bridge   42
    A liberal society   45

Part Two

3   Death and Dying in America   51
    The Philosophers' Brief   52
    The right to die   58

Legal milestones   61
The Oregon Death with Dignity Act   64
The state and the individual revisited   67

4 Legal Disputes over Death in England   80
The Devlin doctrine   80
The Tony Bland case   82
Killing and letting die revisited   85
Euthanasia in 1994 and 2004   88
The Diane Pretty case   89

5 Legalising Euthanasia in The Netherlands   95
The Dutch scene   95
Early euthanasia cases   97
The Rotterdam criteria   99
The Dutch definition of euthanasia   99
The Remmelink reports   101

6 A Legislative Experiment in Australia   114
Withdrawal of treatment – John McEwan to Mrs V   115
Suicide, assisted suicide and voluntary euthanasia   118
Voluntary euthanasia and physician-assisted suicide   120
The Northern Territory experiment   124
The Nancy Crick case 2002   129

Conclusion   135

References   143
Further reading   151
Index   157

Series Preface

The date, the mood of the times, the changed view of what should engage the attention of social philosophers and students of ethics, all combine to suggest that this is the right moment for a book series which aims to make a reasoned contribution to debate about ethical decision-making in many areas of practical policy where the moral map seems unclear and opinion is frequently divided.

To some extent, this is always to be expected, but the start of the third millennium was greeted in the Western world with particular hope and optimism. It was a world eager to put behind it the twentieth century, the first half of which had seen two world wars, the second a period in which the two ideologies of communism and free democracy had remained precariously poised on the brink of mutually assured destruction. The apparent removal of that threat produced a millennial mood of new hope for the future which was reflected in public celebration and a widespread welcome for change; the new, the novel, the innovatory, the modern and the modernising were key words reflecting these aspirations. And indeed the world *did* change, although it took another year or two to reveal that this was not to be in the benevolent way people had hoped. The events in New York of 11 September 2001 and subsequent developments elsewhere in the world produced a seismic shift in the way the world would be viewed, reversing the complacency that had followed the ending of the Cold War. A new religious divide was opening up between a secularised West with its origins in Judaeo-Christian values and an observant Islam; at the same time, religious divisions attached compulsory labels even to the religiously uncommitted.

One consequence of all this is that it has become clear how far Western values, public and private, shifted in the second half of the twentieth century. Even the first half of that century would not have produced such contrasts in values, expectations and behaviour amongst the main cultural divisions of the world. Dress, customs, marriage traditions, women's role, entertainment – in all these areas, a certain commonality would have prevailed, capable of oiling the wheels of cultural contact and exchange. Currently, though, a widening gulf is to be found in views about what is decent or permissible in the private sphere; and this difference in viewpoint expresses itself publicly in the media, in sexual behaviour, in family policy. At the same time, on the broader stage of states, nations and communities, other differences emerge. Old assumptions about the nature, conditions and justifications of war no longer fit the contemporary world, while concepts of ethnic and national identity have become confused. Individuals and groups in a globalised world have voluntarily uprooted themselves, ignoring traditional territorial boundaries and jurisdictions, and this has forced the desirable destinations of the wealthier West to confront contentious questions concerning refugees, immigration and control of borders.

In another sphere again, the world of scientific research and the pursuit of knowledge, Western science – now a world science – has produced advances on many fronts. One of these is in the technology of war and weaponry; another, discoveries in biomedical areas, especially genetics. The first of these generates new fears and a sense of individual helplessness in the face of threats; the second, new ethical questions concerning the margins of life – questions about how to deal with the extending human lifespan and how to regulate the possibilities that have arisen for controlling human life at the embryonic stage. Science has also dramatically changed communication and is certain to go on doing so. Computers will be less mechanistic and more biological. They will also be cheaper and more ubiquitous – people in third world countries as well as in the richer developed world will have access to them.

Again, while wars rage between peoples, there are those who predict that a new war-front that will open up will be that of humans versus other forms of life, perhaps even at the bacterial level. The brief period of human dominance of the planet may be coming to an end, aided and precipitated by our careless treatment of the natural environment. On the one hand, then, some would paint a Malthusian picture of the new era, ending in planetary destruction, possibly precipitated by a self-destructive Armageddon. On the other hand, there remains the inestimable gift of human reason which, if supported by longstanding values that still command widespread respect, may yet lead us out of the current darkness into a second Enlightenment. The questions remain, however, uneasily unanswerable. Will we use scientific and medical advance for good? Will we be able to take a thoughtful and restrained approach to the world environment? Will we choose to embrace the best rather than the worst aspects of the world's religious heritages? Will we be able to retain and indeed reassert the ethical values, public and private, with which these are linked: the private values of love, trust, faithfulness, duty, modesty, unselfishness, respect for one another; the public values of non-licentious freedom, regard for the rights of the human individual and the pursuit of the common good?

A thin strand of optimism suggests that open thought and honest reflection may at least contribute towards finding the right answers to these questions. It is this thin strand of optimism that provides a background and a justification for this series of books, which addresses the ethical dimensions of some key controversies of our time. The authors of books in the series, while varied in their views and positions, seek to set out and analyse the most pressing of today's issues, to offer in some cases their own solutions, but also to provide the arguments that will allow their readers to agree or disagree, for that is the privilege and prerogative of reason.

Acknowledgements

This book has been written while I have been a Research Fellow at the Key Centre for Ethics, Law, Justice and Governance at Griffith University, Brisbane, Queensland, Australia. The Centre specialises in applied ethics, in forging partnerships between 'engaged academics' and 'reflective practitioners', and in road-testing theories. So it was a very appropriate setting for a project on euthanasia – this most applied and universal of issues.

My thanks go to the Director, Professor Charles Sampford, and the Centre Manager, Lynette Farquhar, as well as to colleagues who were supportive by reading material and drawing references of interest to my attention – especially Margaret Palmer, Carmel Connors, Teresa Chataway and Christine Thomson. Christine Thomson also assisted with formatting the text and with the painstaking work of endnotes. Denise Conroy was also a great help in finding reference material.

Thanks go too to the Series Editor, Professor Brenda Almond, and the Editor, Jackie Jones, and staff at Edinburgh University Press.

Finally, I thank my children, Andy and Deb, for their constant love and encouragement.

Gail Tulloch

Part One

Choice and Death

Death, be not proud, though some have called thee
Mighty and dreadful, for thou art not so.

John Donne ('Divine Poems X')

Death comes to all of us. Mortality is the human condition. Yet though we know we will die, we do not know the timing or the manner of our death. The learned consciousness that our time is not infinite adds a fundamental meaning and value to the time we have – an edge that would be missing were we immortal.

As a society, we have a sense of a normal lifespan – whether it be Shakespeare's seven ages of man or the Biblical three score years and ten – and also a sense of the normal stages and tasks at each stage (Erikson's seven-stage model being one of the most influential).[1] This has been extended, due to medical advances which have continuously rescued, saved or cured us of what would have ended our lives in earlier times. Certainly, however, in the normal order of things, no matter how extended the lifespan, parents die before their children.

We have a sense too of a 'good death', though this may have varied throughout history and across cultures – and we hope for it for ourselves, according to our conception of what such a good death is.

So, death is the one great certainty, the defining condition of our life that sharpens the importance of choice. If we do A at the age of twenty-five, we did not do B at that point in time, and cannot rewind our life and redo our actions. This is not something to brood about, but simply an existential boundary condition of being human.

Biological death

At the biological level, for all living organisms, one generation succeeds another and in turn makes way for the next. This is not a cycle of mere repetition. Since Darwin we have come to understand that organisms survive that are best adapted to the prevailing environmental conditions: the fittest survive and environmental mutations occur. Death so understood can be seen as one of nature's ways of improving life – a backdrop for natural selection and new experiments in evolution.

At the non-human level, an animal's heart fails or it ceases breathing; it is then deemed dead. In the normal course of events, excluding accident or injury, higher animals die progressively, from cells and tissues to organs and vital systems, culminating in the collapse of the whole body.

It has long been known that death of all parts of a multicellular organism does not occur simultaneously. As the heart was considered the central organ, its cessation was taken as the beginning of death for other vital organs. Mammalian organisms have nervous, circulatory, respiratory, gastrointestinal, excretory and endocrine systems. Parts of some of these may be damaged for a time without irreversible damage, and there is a hierarchy involved, in that some systems are more vital and time-sensitive than others. Bone may be lost, and a kidney may cease functioning for several hours – indeed, in humans one kidney may cease functioning completely, provided the other remains functioning. But if the heart or lungs stop working only briefly, irreparable damage may occur if intervention does not take place.

Absence of heartbeat and absence of breathing have thus long been taken to be the criteria of clinical death.

Human death

Human death is more multifaceted than mere biological death, however. Human beings know they are mortal, though their level of understanding of this may vary with the level of sophistication of their society. Consciousness of this existential boundary condition defines the human being from an early age; 'the mortal ape' may be a better way to capture human uniqueness than other candidates such as 'the languaging ape' – and certainly better than 'the laughing ape' or 'the territorial ape'. This consciousness of our mortality permeates human psychology and drives culture, myths and religion, being both attempts to reconcile us to, and provide explanations of, this elemental fact in our cosmology.

All our projects are formed and carried out in its shadow, as Andrew Marvell so graphically expressed it in 'To His Coy Mistress':

> Had we but World enough, and Time,
> This coyness Lady were no crime ...
> But at my back I always hear
> Time's winged Chariot hurrying near.

Time is the basic currency of human life; its finitude gives value to the projects we choose, for everything we do is at the cost of something else. We cannot count on another chance to take 'the road not travelled'.

Primitive man's awareness of death was expressed in the worship of fertility and other symbols of life. Death was seen as a transition from one phase of life to another. Burial was a rite of passage like puberty, as the contents of prehistoric tombs indicate. Early religions conceived of the afterlife in more spiritual terms than the Judaeo-Christian tradition. Man is the only creature that buries its dead, and has done so since the dawn of human culture – which may make 'the burying ape' even more apt than 'the mortal ape'.

Neanderthal people buried their dead from 50,000 BC, and Paleolithic people not only buried their dead, but also provided them with food and other equipment they might need, implying a belief in an afterlife. The Greeks and Romans believed the dead had to cross the River Styx to the land of the dead, and hence buried the dead with a coin in the mouth to pay Charon, the ferryman, and a honey cake for Cerberus, the fearsome dog that guarded the gates of Hades (or hell).

Death has been deified, personified, placated by ritual throughout human history, and different rituals are all ways of marking the significance of death and expressing respect for the deceased, as well as giving closure and comfort to the bereaved.

The conception of death in most religions and cultures is tied to a view about the constitution of human nature. On one view, a person is seen as a psychophysical organism, both material and non-material aspects being seen as essential for an integrated personal existence, which death fatally shatters. Some element of the person may survive, but not the essential self or personality. So the ancient Mesopotamians, Hebrews and Greeks held that only a shadowy wraith descended to the realm of the dead.

The Greeks held a dualistic view of the person, comprising an inner, essential self or soul, which is non-material and essentially immortal, and a physical body, separated at death. In Hinduism and Buddhism, the subsequent fate of the soul is determined by the manner in which it has lived that life.

On the other hand, in religions which envisage an effective afterlife, such as that of the ancient Egyptians, and in Judaism, Zoroastrianism, Christianity and Islam, reconstitution or resurrection of the body is involved, to restore the psychophysical complex of personality.

The good death

Religion, culture and myth are all, therefore, important in shaping the view of death in a society, or in sub-groups within a society. In a modern Western society, death is very often depersonalised, taking place away from home in a hospital setting, often involving machines and a heavily drugged patient. The hospice movement, founded by Dame Cicely Saunders, and the pioneering work of Dr Elizabeth Kübler-Ross, offered a different story. At an individual level, a person who faces death has been understood as undergoing five stages.[2] The first stage is denial, as the person responds with shock rather than accepting their finiteness and the reality of their oncoming death. The second stage is anger, which can be displaced onto nursing and medical staff, family members and even God. The third stage is bargaining, where the patient makes an offer in exchange for temporary prolongation of life. This is a stage of truce psychologically speaking, and when it is up, the patient moves to the fourth stage, depression. Having faced the certainty that life is coming to an end and having responded to losses already experienced in coming to this point, the patient descends into a deep and silent depression, called the preparatory grief, and begins to separate from the living, finally wanting only next of kin by the bedside. The final stage is one of acceptance, and if no extraordinary means are used to prolong life, the patient is prepared to die with peace and dignity, and experience a good death. For patients to reach this final stage of equanimity, they need excellent nursing care with adequate pain relief, flexible management, to allow satisfaction of simple needs, and a hospital staff and family who accept the reality that the patient is dying and can talk about it, if and when the patient expresses the desire to do so.

Family members and attending staff may also proceed through these five stages. Those who lose a loved one suddenly and unexpectedly may go through adjustment after the death occurs, often requiring more time to reach the stage of acceptance. It is not uncommon for widows and widowers to die soon after the death of their spouse in the course of their own grief process, which may make them more vulnerable to death, often without reaching the stage of acceptance.

A 'good death' may thus be seen as involving sufficient time for all concerned – patient and family – to reach the stage of acceptance. This is where palliative care comes into its own. The outcome may be the same, but there is all the difference in the world between a sudden and unexpected and untimely death in an Intensive Care Ward, with an unconscious or barely conscious patient connected to machines and tubes, and a timely death, where patient and family have seen the writing on the wall and the patient's deterioration, and accepted that death is a better alternative and is indeed timely.

Defining death

As noted earlier, absence of heartbeat and absence of breathing were long taken as the defining criteria that determined death.[3] However, in 1968 the Ad Hoc Committee of the Harvard Medical School recommended that irreversible coma, or brain death, be taken as the new criterion for death: a comatose patient with a permanently non-functioning brain, non-responsive to external stimuli and showing no spontaneous respiration, muscular movements or cephalic reflexes, with no brain waves, should be regarded as dead. The condition must have been present for twenty-four hours. The test case was Karen Quinlan, who lived for eight years after her respirator was switched off.

This was a momentous change, brought about by persistent vegetative state patients and the pressures of organ donation. There remain some problems of irreversibility, as in the astonishing case of Terry Wallis, an Arkansas man who woke after nineteen years in a coma.[4]

It is often difficult to establish a moment of death, outside the 'ER' scenario familiar from television, when the monitor flatlines. Yet it is clearly necessary to have this determinateness, for both legal reasons and the medical implications of ensuring that an organ for transplant is being removed from a donor who is indeed clinically dead.

Common sense would suggest that what counts as dead for a human being is the same as what counts as dead for a horse, a dog, a budgerigar, a fish, a tree – 'the permanent cessation of the flow of vital bodily fluids', whether they be blood or sap. There is a vicious circularity and double-dipping involved, however, as Singer has pointed out.[5] How do you tell if a body fluid is vital? By seeing if the being dies when this fluid stops flowing. And how do we know if the being has died? Again, by seeing if its vital bodily fluids have stopped flowing.

Black's *Law Dictionary* (1968) gives a classic definition of death which avoids this problem of circularity by being more comprehensive:

> Death: The cessation of life; the ceasing to exist, defined by physicians as a total stoppage of the circulation of the blood, and a cessation of the animal and vital functions consequent thereupon, such as respiration, pulsation, etc.[6]

This definition has the common-sense virtue of applying to both humans and animals. On this definition, once breathing and circulation cease, after an interval the patient is dead. Theory and practice were in accord. So what disrupted this status quo?[7] In December 1967 there occurred the pioneering transplant of a human heart into Louis Washkansky by Dr Christian Barnard in South Africa. Although Washkansky died eighteen days later, within a year more than a hundred such operations had been attempted, adding further pressure to a problem that had been brewing since the development of the respirator in response to the worldwide poliomyelitis epidemic of the 1950s. A Danish doctor solved the problem of polio-stricken children dying because they could not breathe by using airbags to pump oxygen into their lungs manually. Then a mechanical pump was attached to the airbag. Respirators were soon common, saving the lives of many people, many of whom needed only temporary help. But what of patients who remained alive, whose hearts continued to beat but who stayed unconscious, perhaps indefinitely? The person could never recover consciousness and was gone forever, but was not dead. Intensive care units experienced the same problem, with the prospect of wards full of permanently unconscious patients.

Barnard's breakthrough exacerbated this situation by opening up the possibility of heart transplants. Whereas kidney transplants had become almost commonplace, they involved no problems about death, because kidneys can be taken from a patient whose heart has stopped. With a heart transplant, however, the heart must be removed as soon as possible after the donor has died. Permanently unconscious patients suddenly became potential life-savers for other patients; but to remove the heart of a still-living patient was murder.[8]

The Harvard definition of brain death

This was the context for the deliberation of the Harvard Brain Death Committee, originally asked for 'further consideration of the definition of death' in the area of kidney transplantation, and affected by the South African heart transplant. The Committee's primary purpose was to define irreversible coma and a new criterion of death, because irreversibly comatose patients were a burden on families and hospitals and because obsolete criteria for the definition of death can lead to controversy in obtaining organs for transplants.[9]

The ethical problem was thus technology-generated. As Dr Beecher, Chairman of the Harvard Brain Death Committee, put it:

> At what ever level we choose to call death, it is an arbitrary decision. Death of the heart? The hair still grows. Death of the brain? The heart may still beat. The need is to choose an irreversible state where the brain no longer functions. It is best to choose a level where, although the brain is dead, usefulness of other organs is still present. This we have tried to make clear in what we have called the new definition of death.[10]

Recall that the Harvard Committee was originally established in the context of ethics of experimentation.

Their report also refers to 'permanent loss of intellect', and 'irreversible coma as a result of permanent brain damage' which was not identical with the death of the whole brain. A permanent vegetative state results from damage to parts of the brain responsible for consciousness, but the brain stem and central nervous system continue to function. Persistent vegetative state patients are not regarded as dead. The reasons given by the Harvard Committee for redefining death apply to all who are irretrievably comatose and not just brain dead – that is, the burden on patients' families and hospitals, and the loss of the opportunity to harvest organs for transplantation. Why, then, did the Committee confine itself to those with no brain activity at all?[11] At that time, before developments in imaging referred to later in this chapter (p. 18), there was no reliable way of telling whether a coma was irreversible unless there was no brain activity at all. But whereas people whose whole brain is dead will stop breathing after they are taken off a respirator, people in a persistent vegetative state may breathe without mechanical assistance. It would be too hard to call such a patient dead and to bury a breathing patient. Terry Wallis, the Arkansas man who came out of a coma after nineteen years and spoke to his mother, then asked for a Pepsi and then milk, is a graphic example of this.

The Harvard redefinition became consensus in fifteen countries, but not Japan, and in 1981 the United States President's Commission for the Study of Ethical Problems in Medicine commented: 'no case has yet been found that met these criteria and regained any brain function'. This Commission completed the Harvard Committee's work in a report titled 'Defining Death'.

The progress of organ transplantation was a factor in the ready adoption of the Harvard definition of death as brain death.[12] Neither the pro-life movement nor the Roman Catholic Church offered the opposition that might have been expected. Singer points to the importance of Pope Pius XII's acknowledgement that the determination of death is for doctors to decide, and argues that the pro-life lobby was worried that support for turning off the respirator of brain dead patients might escalate into other areas, such as euthanasia. Two pro-life advocates, Germain Grisez and Joseph Boyle, argued that an organism is 'a co-ordinated system' and that because the brain is the organ that maintains the dynamic equilibrium of the system, death occurs when the functioning of the whole brain is irreversibly lost. This substituted for the earlier view of the heart as central.[13]

Singer finds this attempted theoretical base unconvincing, because the function of the brain can be replaced, just like the role of the kidney or heart. The later cases of Trisha Marshall (1993) and Marion Ploch (1992) – two brain dead pregnant women who were maintained alive for three and a half months and five months, respectively, for the sake of the foetuses they were carrying – show this.

Marion Ploch was an eighteen-year-old German woman who suffered a fractured skull when the car she was travelling in hit a tree. Her parents were told their daughter was in intensive care and would not survive, and were asked to donate her organs – which they refused to do. Then it was discovered that Marion was pregnant and the doctors asked to maintain her bodily functions for another five months at which time the foetus could survive. The case became a *cause célèbre* in the popular press, as the parents sought to have the respirator turned off. Singer argues that part of the furore came from resistance to the idea that she really was dead. If she was dead, how could turning off the respirator allow her to 'die with dignity'? The pregnancy spontaneously miscarried a month later, but the reason is unknown, as the parents refused to allow an autopsy.

Trisha Marshall's case raised similar issues. In April 1993 she broke into a disabled man's apartment and demanded money, but was shot in the head and declared brain dead two days later in the Intensive Care Unit of Highland General Hospital, San Francisco. She was seventeen weeks pregnant, and both her boyfriend (she had four other children) and her parents wanted the hospital to make every effort to allow the baby to be born. The ethics committee of Highland Hospital tried to act in the interest of the foetus, despite public criticism of the cost involved. In August a baby boy was born by caesarean section, and after three and a half weeks in intensive care went to Marshall's family, after a custody dispute with the boyfriend, who was proved by blood test not to be the father.

Before these two cases, however, the only countering evidence that a brain dead patient could live longer than a few days came from the Japanese in a 1986 study of the results of giving an antidiuretic hormone to brain dead patients. Rather than dying in a day or so, they lived up to twenty-three days. Later studies have shown that the bodily functions of brain dead patients can be maintained as long as 201 days, so in this sense, modern medicine is replacing even the coordinating role of the brain.

It is, then, not the integrative or coordinating role of the brain that makes its death the end of everything we value, but its association with our consciousness and person.[14] As Beecher indicates, there is no 'fact of the matter'. If we choose to mark death at any moment short of the body being stiff and cold, we are really making an ethical judgement, for a particular purpose.

The acceptance of the Harvard brain death definition is a solid bioethical achievement, combining clear thinking, medical practice and community acceptance. However, that was not the end of the matter because many people, even doctors and nurses, do not think of brain dead people as really dead. Brain death, Singer argues, is a convenient fiction that enabled us to salvage organs and withdraw medical treatment that is doing no good. Two problems remain, related, not surprisingly, to advances in medical knowledge and technology. Even when tests show that brain death has occurred, some brain functions remain – and not only the antidiuretic hormone that the Japanese replaced by a drip. Blood pressure may rise and the heartbeat quicken when patients are cut open to remove their organs, which suggests the brain is still regulating the body.[15]

It seems desirable to bring the definition of brain death into line with current medical practice. Which functions of the brain are we to take as marking the difference between life and death? One more metamorphosis takes us to the present and to the notion of cortical death – death of the higher brain, which regulates consciousness.

A few brief facts about the brain and its functions may help to show what is at issue here.

The brain

The most ancient part of the brain is the brain stem, which controls the basic functions of breathing, heart rate and blood pressure, and links the spinal cord to the newer part of the brain, the cerebrum, which contains the cerebral hemispheres which control the intellect and will, and the thalamus and limbic system, which organises moods, memory and appetite, emotion and feeling.

The limbic, old mammalian brain was an addition to the brain inherited from reptilian ancestors. The reptilian brain comprised the upper brain stem, including the hypothalamus, and regulated stereotyped instinctive behaviour and vital biological functions and rhythms. In modern mammals, it is surrounded by the neocortex – the new mammalian brain which is the site of reasoning and, in man, of language. The higher up the evolutionary scale, the larger the neocortex is in relation to the limbic brain.

The cerebrum is the third area of the brain and is the largest proportion of the brain in man. The outer layer, the cerebral cortex, is folded more tightly in man than in other animals, which enables more information to be stored, and so is related to intelligence.

In most adults, the speech centres are limited to the left hemisphere. About fifteen per cent of left-handers and two per cent of right-handers have speech on both sides. Some left-handers develop speech on the left, but fewer than half have it on the right. In left-handers the two halves are not as specialised. In the young, each side probably has the potential for speech and language, but dominance for speech and other skills is firmly established by the age of ten and cannot be transferred.

The difference in abilities between the two cerebral hemispheres seems unique to human beings, the right hemisphere being the artistic brain. Our knowledge of the hemisphere functions was dramatically increased in the 1970s by the work of Roger Sperry, the Californian neurosurgeon who had done original laboratory research on animals and who pioneered a radical new treatment to prevent epileptic seizures, by cutting through the corpus collosum, between the two hemispheres. His split brain operation, featured in a television documentary 'The Mind of Man', created two minds, one verbal, analytic and dominant, the other artistic but mute. In a version of Kim's Game, objects were placed on a tray and screened from the subject. The subject could respond to verbal commands only with the right side of the body, which is under the direction of the left hemisphere. If the subject held an object, hidden from her view, in her right hand, she could say what it was; if it were held in her left hand, she could not say what it was, but could pick it out. The sight of the hand groping blindly over the tray was very dramatic.

Normally, the two halves continue to interact, even when severed, but the subtle effects of the surgery showed up under the battery of post-operative evaluative tests. It is both obvious and significant that intelligence tests evaluate left hemisphere activity and educational assessment is heavily biased towards the rational, the linear, the analytical.

Defining death: selective non-treatment of severely disabled newborns

The next step in understanding the move towards a definition of death as cortical death comes from an examination of the issue of selective non-treatment of severely disabled newborns, which may be regarded as medical infanticide, as judgements of futility of treatment became augmented by considerations of quality of life, centring on cortical function.[16]

The problem arose in the UK in the 1950s, in relation to the treatment of spina bifida (divided spine, bifurcated spine) babies, almost all of whom died after birth until the advent of antibiotics, which enabled doctors to drain cerebra-spinal fluid which would otherwise have built up in the brain. Dr Lorber,[17] a paediatrician in Sheffield, was initially enthusiastic about the new treatment and wrote an article with two colleagues, advocating that infants with spina bifida be operated on as soon as possible. The operation to close the open wound at the base of the spine was not all that was required, however, and frequently had to be followed by surgery on the spine and hip. After a decade Lorber analysed the records of the 848 cases actively treated at Sheffield and found such poor outcomes (e.g. in length of survival) that he suggested a more selective policy, of treating only infants without 'adverse' criteria. The majority of spina bifida babies would then not be treated: no antibiotics should be given in case of infection and they would not be tube-fed. They should only be kept comfortable and free from pain – few were then likely to live more than six months.

The practice swung away from universal intervention, even where less severe conditions were concerned. This was endorsed in four British court decisions. In one, John Pearson, a baby with Down's syndrome, was prescribed painkilling drugs and nursing care only, and died within four days. At the trial of the doctor involved, Leonard Arthur, in 1981, the charge of murder was reduced to attempted murder, since it was found that other medical factors could have been the cause of death, and not the treatment he had initiated (see too p. 27). The question of intent was also considered, and the action endorsed by experts. The doctor was found not guilty.

The Baby Doe case[18] was a similarly high-profile case in the US. Baby Doe was born in 1982 with Down's syndrome and a blockage of his digestive system. Without an operation, he would starve. His physician, Dr Owen, opposed such an operation, and the baby died while the case was before the court. The Reagan government policy was that providers of healthcare receiving federal funds must not discriminate against the handicapped, and 'Baby Doe squads' were set up to investigate complaints. The guidelines proved unworkable and the economic costs (US$400,000 for a baby with a zero chance of a normal life expectancy) were high. The guidelines went to court before Judge Gessell and were struck down: futile treatment would not be required.

In 1984, the Final Rule was that only medically beneficial treatment would be required. The American Medical Association took the rule to court and it was found invalid. The Reagan administration appealed to the Supreme Court, which also struck down the regulation and found that medical decisions should be left to the parents, informed by the medical team.

In contrast, in Melbourne in 1986, Judge Vincent ordered life-sustaining treatment in a similar case of a baby born with a severe disability, on the basis that 'the law does not permit decisions to be made concerning the quality of life nor any assessment of the value of any human being'. This reflected the view that life is an irreducible value and quality of life in a particular case cannot be taken into account.

Another Australian case concerned Baby M, who was born with severe spina bifida. She was likely to be paralysed in the lower legs, unable to walk, incontinent, with the risk of mental retardation and epilepsy. Her parents were Roman Catholics. Dr Loughnan, the attending paediatrician at the Royal Children's Hospital, Melbourne, recommended not operating to close the lesion on her spine, nor treating the excess fluid on her brain. She was given a painkiller and a sedative, and fed on demand but not via a tube. Five days later, the police visited the hospital at the behest of the Right to Life Association, an anti-abortion group, alerted by the baby's great-aunt. The police were satisfied that the treatment was appropriate after examination by the police doctor and other specialists. Ten days after birth, she developed respiratory problems and was given morphine. She died two days later. The death was reported to the coroner because of the police involvement and media interest.

An inquest two years later found the treatment was 'legally, ethically and morally sound' and condemned the intervention by the Right to Life Association. The practice of selective non-treatment was based on assessments of medical futility and quality of life, and followed the UK experience.

Similar considerations were evident in 1989, in Chicago, when Rudy Linares took a gun into the hospital ward and disconnected tubes from his infant son, Samuel, who had swallowed a balloon at the age of seven months. It had lodged in his windpipe and he had been without oxygen for too long, and lapsed into a coma. He was put on a respirator and eight months later there had been no improvement. His family asked for the respirator to be turned off, but the hospital refused. His father Rudy took a gun into the ward, disconnected Samuel, and cradled him in his arms for thirty minutes until he died. Rudy then gave himself up. He was charged with murder. The grand jury however would not issue an indictment for homicide. The medical examiner ruled that the death was accidental and had occurred when Samuel swallowed the balloon. Disagreeing with medical staff evidence that the infant was not brain dead, the medical examiner concluded:

> The person was dead. The only thing you kept living was the organs.[19]

Rudy Linares was charged over a misdemeanour with a weapon. The judge gave him a suspended sentence and wished him luck.

These cases show the importance of judges, juries and public opinion in different jurisdictions, and the way harsh legislative penalties have often been modified in the direction of compassion and common sense in practice.

This was not so, however, with a particularly excruciating problem which turned on the issue of cortical death and the availability of organs for transplant in relation to a tragic category of patients – anencephalic and cortically dead infants.[20]

In 1991 in Melbourne, at the Royal Children's Hospital, a conference was held on Anencephalics, Infants and Brain Death: Treatment Options and the Issue of Organ Donation. It was sponsored by the Victorian Law Commission as well as the hospital, supported by the Attorney General, and picketed by the Right to Life Association. It was attended by bioethicist Peter Singer,[21] as an invited panel member, along with another philosopher, two lawyers, a paediatrician and an intensive care specialist. This 'consensus development panel' was to consider the moral status of two problematic categories of newborns: anencephalics ('no brain') babies, who have only a brain stem, and cortically dead babies. Neither will ever become conscious, yet both can live a long time in intensive care. The cortically dead infant is not brain dead because the legal definition of brain death (in the UK and Australia) requires that the whole brain has ceased to function. Anencephalic babies usually die within a few hours, and only one per cent survive for three months, without efforts to keep them alive.

The Director of the ICU, Dr Shann, described the case of a baby boy with severe heart disease who had been put on a ventilator and given continual drugs to keep him alive, and whose outlook was hopeless. In the next bed was a baby who had a bleed into his brain, which had destroyed his cerebral cortex. He could not survive off the ventilator, but was not legally dead:

> There was therefore one child who was completely normal except for a dying heart in one bed, and in the next bed, a child with a dead brain cortex but a normal heart. As it happened, the two children had the same blood group, so the heart of the child with no cerebral cortex could have been transplanted into the child with cardiomyopathy [heart disease].[22]

Within a short time, both babies were dead. No other option was available legally in Australia or anywhere else in the world at that time, as two examples from America and Italy illustrate.

The year after the Royal Children's Hospital conference, Laura Campo of Florida was told in the eighth month of pregnancy that her foetus was anencephalic. By this stage it was too late for an abortion. (Due to lack of medical insurance, she had not attended a doctor before that time.) She decided to have a caesarean birth, so her baby would be born alive and could be an organ donor.

Baby Theresa was born on 21 March 1992 with some brain stem function. Because she was not dead, it was not possible to remove any organs. Laura Campo went to court to try to get permission, but the judge refused. She and Justin Pearson, the baby's father, went on the Don Lane Show on television, seeking a change in Florida's laws on brain death. The baby deteriorated after nine days, the respirator was removed and she died.

A similar case occurred two weeks later in Italy, where parents of anencephalic Baby Valentina were refused permission by an Italian court to make her organs available. She also died soon after the court's decision.

This was the excruciating problem which had precipitated the Royal Children's Hospital conference. Dr Shann argued that the cortex was the organ that mattered. Without it there is permanent loss of consciousness, no person, no personality, even though the heart may still be beating and breathing movements occurring. He suggested it should be legal to use organs from the body of a cortically dead person.

Who, though, would be prepared to bury such a body, particularly that of a newborn?[23]

Dr Robert Truog, from the Intensive Care Unit at Harvard Medical School, supported Dr Shann, stating 'death is the irreversible loss of the capacity for consciousness'.

The nightmare prospect that such a cortically dead or permanent vegetative state patient may wake up was addressed by Dr Margaret de Campo, a radiologist at the Royal Children's Hospital; advances in imaging the brain mean that it was now possible to detect in what areas of the brain the blood is still flowing. Without blood flow, the capacity for consciousness has been irretrievably lost and so the spectre of making the mistake of premature burial or cremation of a patient who might recover could not occur. (This kind of imaging is now routinely used in studies of addiction, anger, anxiety and Alzheimer's disease.)[24]

Once again, technical developments had impacted on ethical dilemmas,[25] as imaging enabled empirical certainty which dissolved a potent objection, and organ donation pressures forced the issue.

The considerations thrown up at the 1991 Melbourne conference do show a development in thinking from a focus on the whole brain as a criterion of death to a more refined focus on cortical death as a justification for ending life.

However, in relation to anencephalic and brain dead infants, there was no change. Peter Singer describes the three options facing the panel:[26] declare such infants legally dead; not declare them dead and therefore not allow them to become organ donors; or allow them to become organ donors, although they are not legally dead. The panel recommended the Victorian Law Reform Commission undertake community consultation. This did not happen, as the Labor Government of Victoria lost office in 1992 and the incoming Liberal Government abolished the Law Reform Commission. It remained illegal in Victoria and anywhere else in the world to use anencephalic and cortically dead infants as organ donors.[27]

In 1989 the Danish Council of Ethics posed three questions that clearly separate the issues involved, but also show the pressure for organ donation that drove the questions:[28]

• When does a human being die?
• When is it permissible to stop trying to keep a human being alive?
• When is it permissible to remove organs from a human being for the purpose of transplantation to another human being?

What other answer could be given to the third question, if the answer is not 'when the human being is dead', or if the goalposts are shifted in adjudicating that.

These questions were posed in the context of a report to Parliament at a time when Denmark was the only country in Western Europe that had not adopted a brain-based criterion of death. In 1990 a law was passed that brought Denmark into line with other European countries and adopted brain death as the criterion of death.[29]

As previously stated, the considerations thrown up at the Melbourne conference show a development in thinking from a focus on the whole brain to a more refined focus on cortical death as both a criterion of death and a justification for ending life.

This thinking was apparent in the UK too in the 1989 case of Tony Bland, where the issue was not one of possible organ transplantation but of letting die. The case is discussed at length in chapter 5. In brief, Tony Bland had been caught in a crush of spectators at Hillsborough Football Stadium. His lungs were compressed and his brain deprived of oxygen. He was in a persistent vegetative state, maintained by artificial hydration and nutrition via a nasogastric tube. In 1992 the Airedale Hospital petitioned the High Court for permission to withdraw artificial feeding and hydration. The case was appealed up to the House of Lords, who significantly found that artificial hydration and feeding were medical treatments, and that a doctor had no duty to continue treatment where it would be of no benefit, and particularly where it was invasive and consent had not been given.

What was of particular significance was that nine judges (one in the Family Division of the High Court, three in the Court of Appeal, and five in the House of Lords) all made it clear they did not value human life that is life in only a biological sense.

Peter Singer hailed the decision as a breach in the sanctity of life doctrine, as here British law formally abandoned the idea that life itself is a benefit, irrespective of its quality, and held rather that for life to be of benefit to the person living it, that person must, as a minimum, have some capacity for awareness or consciousness.

Singer had had misgivings about the notion of whole-brain death, which he felt was 'something of a deception, an ethical choice masquerading as medical fact'. Moreover, the definition did not apply to persistent vegetative state patients. This made the Tony Bland case decision, in Singer's view, 'perhaps the most important decision of the twentieth century on the law relating to the sanctity of human life'.

The whole brain definition of death may not be ideal, but it is an improvement on the traditional view that preceded it. It is still contentious – not least because of pressure to extend it to a cortical definition, despite problems with declaring dead people who are pink and warm and breathing – but is where the boundary is set at the moment.

This chapter has examined the concept of death, from biological death to human death, and its evolution from primitive times to the traditional conception of death being the cessation of heartbeat and breathing. It then traced the emergence of the Harvard definition of death as brain death in response to the challenge posed by medical developments, as patients were increasingly being able to be kept alive, and the demands of organ transplantation became more pressing.

It then traced the emergence of a new criterion of death – cortical death – after analysing the structure and functions of the brain, and the importance for human identity of the functions of consciousness located in the cortex.

The selective non-treatment of severely disabled newborns exemplified the nexus between futility of treatment and quality of life in two situations: cessation of treatment and potential organ donation. The organ donation prospect remained morally unacceptable, but considerations of cortical death did come to play a role in judgements as to cessation of treatment, not only of severely disabled newborns, but also, with the Tony Bland case, for persistent vegetative state patients.

Notes

1. E. H. Erikson, *Childhood and Society* (New York: W. W. Norton, 1950), p. 219; E. H. Erikson, *Identity, Youth and Crisis* (New York: W. W. Norton, 1968).
2. E. Kübler-Ross, *On Death and Dying* (London: Routledge, 1989).
3. C. M. Culver and B. Gert, 'The Definition and Criterion of Death', in *Biomedical Ethics*, ed. T. A. Mappes and J. Zembaty (New York: McGraw-Hill, 1991).
4. Bill Hoffmann, 'Coma Man Awakes from 19-Year Slumber', *New York Post*, No. 10 (July 2003).
5. P. Singer, *Rethinking Life and Death* (Melbourne: Text, 1994), p. 21.
6. Ibid.
7. President's Commission for the Study of Ethical Problems in Medicine and Biomedical and Behavioural Research, 'Why "Update" Death?', in *Biomedical Ethics*, ed. T. Mappes and J. Zembaty (New York: McGraw-Hill, 1981).
8. L. H. Kerridge, 'Death, Dying and Donation: Organ Transplantation and the Dignity of Death', *Issues in Law and Medicine* Vol. 18, No. 1 (2002).
9. National Health and Medical Research Council (NHMRC), 'Certifying Death: The Brain Function Criterion' (1997); National Health and Medical Research Council (NHMRC), 'Donating Organs after Death: Ethical Issues' (1997).
10. Singer, *Rethinking Life and Death*, p. 26.
11. D. Hershenov, 'The Problematic Role of Irreversibility in the Definition of Death', *Bioethics* Vol. 17, No. 1 (2003).
12. P. McCullagh, 'Euthanasia and Attitudes towards Others: Why is it an Issue Now?', in *Euthanasia, Palliative and Hospice Care and the Terminally Ill*, ed. J. Stuparich (Canberra: Right to Life Association, 1992).
13. Singer, *Rethinking Life and Death*, p. 30.

14. D. Persson, 'Human Death – a View from the Beginning of Life', *Bioethics* Vol. 16, No. 1 (2002).

15. NHMRC, 'Certifying Death: The Brain Function Criterion'.

16. K. Street et al., 'The Decision Making Process Regarding the Withdrawal or Withholding of Potential Life-Saving Treatments in a Children's Hospital', *Journal of Medical Ethics* Vol. 26, No. 5 (2000).

17. W. Molloy, *Vital Choices* (Harmondsworth: Penguin, 1994); Singer, *Rethinking Life and Death*, p. 115.

18. J. E. Frader, 'Baby Doe Blinders', *JAMA* Vol. 284, No. 6 (September 2000); R. T. Clark Jr, 'Baby Jose', *JAMA* Vol. 284, No. 9 (2000); M. L. Gross, 'Avoiding Anomalous Newborns: Preemptive Abortion Treatment Thresholds and the Case of Baby Messenger', *Journal of Medical Ethics* 26, No. 4 (2000).

19. Singer, *Rethinking Life and Death*, p. 115.

20. M. Cuttini et al., 'End-of-Life Decisions in Neonatal Intensive Care: Physician's Self-Reported Practices in 7 European Countries', *The Lancet* Vol. 355, No. 17 (June 2000).

21. Singer, *Rethinking Life and Death*, pp. 38ff.

22. Ibid., pp. 41–2.

23. M. Sklansky, 'Neonatal Euthanasia: Moral Considerations and Criminal Liability', *Journal of Medical Ethics* Vol. 27, No. 1 (2001).

24. Hershenov, 'The Problematic Role of Irreversibility in the Definition of Death'.

25. C. Seale, 'Changing Patterns of Death and Dying', *Social Science and Medicine* Vol. 51 (2000).

26. Singer, *Rethinking Life and Death*, p. 52.

27. H. E. McHaffie, 'Withholding/Withdrawing Treatment from Neonates: Legislation and Official Guidelines across Europe', *Journal of Medical Ethics* Vol. 25, No. 6 (1999).

28. Singer, *Rethinking Life and Death*, p. 55.

29. M. L. Gross, 'Abortion and Neonaticide: Ethics, Practice and Policy in 4 Nations', *Bioethics* Vol. 16, No. 3 (2002).

2

Stark Choices

In chapter 1 we explored the concept of death, from biological death to human death, and the way conceptions of human death have changed in response to the challenges posed by medical developments which generated problematic cases. Two such landmark cases were Karen Quinlan in 1975, and Tony Bland in 1993.

This chapter casts a broader net, to show the pressures that built up in various places around troubling cases and the varying approaches that were taken to the stark choices such cases presented. Little by little, boundaries were extended, but in a painful and piecemeal way, with semantic twists and turns that show the pressure of the task of accommodating public opinion to medical practices and legislative policies concerning euthanasia.

The cases in chapter 1 highlighted the right to die, via cessation of treatment, and the problematic treatment and selective non-treatment of severely damaged babies, which may be called medical infanticide as much as euthanasia.

The 1970s began and ended with significant cases of people wanting to die, or wanting assisted suicide. Karen Quinlan was the first celebrated 'right to die' case, when her parents wanted cessation of treatment and finally succeeded in having her taken off a respirator. To everyone's surprise she continued to breathe normally and lived a further eight years. The cost to her family resonates from the sad inscription on her gravestone:

> Born 20 July 1957
> Departed 11 Jan 1983
> At Peace 26 Dec 1990

It was a time of confusion, makeshift, ad hoc decisions, flux, ambivalence and uncertainty in this and other areas of biomedicine. Turning to the 1980s, Nancy Cruzan was also a 'right to die' case, whose parents were asking not merely for the respirator to be switched off, but the feeding tube to be taken out, which was even more controversial as it raised the question of what was medical treatment and what was basic care and nutrition. (The issue was raised again in 2003 in Victoria, in a case which involved the Public Advocate.[1]) The Cruzan case finally turned on the inference from evidence (though second-hand) that this is what she would have wanted.

The prevailing impression left by the review of these cases is surely one of repetition rather than of resolution. Problematic 'right to die' cases comprise an extension of the right to refuse treatment, early established on one's own behalf, provided 'wittingness' was established and one had provided competent, voluntarily informed consent, to more contested cases involving the right to refuse treatment on behalf of another. With Karen Quinlan, the treatment refused was clearly medical – a respirator; with Nancy Cruzan the context was the more problematic one of nutrition – of removing a feeding tube – and the inference was needed that she would have wanted this action.

At both ends of the lifespan there were problems – with euthanasia and with not treating damaged infants – and a slide from patients who were conscious and competent, to conscious but incompetent patients, and then to unconscious patients.

Just as there was evolution in the concept of death, as outlined in chapter 1, so too there was evolution in the discussion of euthanasia.

A series of conceptual distinctions was drawn to try to chart a way forward, a series of binary oppositions, with one alternative being less reprehensible.

Conceptual distinctions

Ordinary/extraordinary

One of those distinctions was between ordinary and extraordinary methods of treatment. This may seem arbitrary, as in ordinary or extraordinary treatment in the Karen Quinlan case. Why is a respirator extraordinary and a feeding tube merely allowing food and nutrition ordinary? Because it is more high-tech? Because it is newer? Given the frequency of use of ventilators, such treatment has become ordinary. Will the 'ordinary/extraordinary measures' distinction really bear much weight? Apart from the obvious fact that yesterday's 'extraordinary' becomes normalised to today's 'ordinary', the very drawing of the distinction is arbitrary and question-begging. What the repudiation of 'extraordinary means' seeks to capture is also expressed as the repudiation of 'heroic measures' (as in the 1976 Peggy Stinson case) – intrusive, depersonalising, high-tech, mechanical intervention that make the patient merely the intersection of various data monitoring systems.

There can be no more graphic example of this than Engelbert Schucking's 'Death at a New York Hospital' account, in Margaret Somerville's *Death Talk*,[2] of the medical procedures imposed on his partner, who had a kidney ailment and home dialysis, and was admitted to a hospital, despite their misgivings, after he rang her doctor concerning an infection she had developed. Despite her living will opposing respiration, she was put on a respirator and subjected to pericardiocentesis (draining fluid from the sac surrounding the heart) – a potentially lethal and terrifying procedure. Despite his legal authority to act on her behalf, his protests were ignored.

It is this situation that is repudiated in so many advance directives, living wills, 'do not resuscitate' orders, but, as Dr William Molloy points out,[3] it is better to specify what measures one would and would not find acceptable, rather than to rely on such a vague, arbitrary, subjective, intuitive distinction. As Dr Lorber's change of heart about the wisdom of treating severely disabled spina bifida babies demonstrates, even 'ordinary' measures such as antibiotics are ruled out – and antibiotics are surely commonplace rather than 'extraordinary' in today's medical practice. Indeed, now the complaint is often made that they are over-used.

In the case of Peggy Stinson, who unsuccessfully asked for no heroic measures for her premature baby who was put on a respirator, the distinction has a point, as it did in the Karen Quinlan case. But in many other cases, it is not this distinction but another that seems to be involved – the 'killing/letting die' distinction.

Killing/letting die

In situations where the pressure is on to avoid the pejorative con-notations of 'killing', and the especially pejorative connotations of 'murder', 'letting die' seemed a good candidate to demarcate those sympathetic cases which we did not want to classify as 'killing', with all the legal ramifications that ensue. Withdrawing treatment, as in the Karen Quinlan and Nancy Cruzan cases, or not commencing it, in the case of severely disabled spina bifida babies under the selective treatment regime, was well captured under the 'letting die' rubric – so putting a much more accept-able face on allowing patients to 'succumb' to death. The same euphemistic language is used in the case of surplus IVF embryos, and has grounded a pragmatic argument for allowing them to be used in stem cell research.

The neutral term would be 'bringing about death'. 'Killing' has stronger negative connotations, and 'murder' clearly means 'wrongful killing' – killing not extenuated by the exemptions of war or self-defence, or weakened to 'manslaughter'. Still, cir-cularity and an element of question-begging and semantic rela-belling seem to be involved.

If the killing/letting die distinction were simply to track the distinction between acts and omissions, then an agent who turns off a life-sustaining machine kills B, while an agent who refrains from putting C on a life-saving machine merely allows C to die.

Is this conclusion plausible? It is more plausible to argue that killing is initiating a series of events that leads to death, whereas allowing to die is not intervening in a course of events that leads to death. This would mean that giving a lethal injection would be killing, whereas not putting a patient on a respirator or taking her off would be allowing to die.

Is the distinction morally significant? Is killing always worse than allowing to die?

It has been argued that there is a significant difference, that where treatment is extraordinary or burdensome, this amounts to 'letting die'. Where the withdrawal of treatment causally results in death, this need not be seen as intentional termination of life and therefore not passive euthanasia, but merely letting die, or 'letting nature take its course'. Though common, this does not seem to me to be a good argument, as I shall argue later.

Furthermore, as Kuhse has argued,[4] in the case of euthanasia, either to kill or to let die is to deprive someone of life. The usual presumption is that it is in one's best interest to continue to live. In the euthanasia context, it is arguable that death, not life, is in the best interest of the person; therefore killing C does not harm C, but rather benefits her positively, while letting C die merely allows benefits to befall C.

Is letting die, rather, avoidance of pointless and painful treatment? In some cases, yes, and then it must be shown that it is the disease that caused the patient's death, but in others, no. Where there are means to treat, then it is the failure to treat, not the disease, that is the cause of death. It must then be shown that the action was undertaken with the intention of causing death. This can easily be denied – and so leads into the double effect justification. This was presumably the reason for the acquittal of Dr Leonard Arthur on the charge of attempted murder in 1980 (see p. 15). Dr Arthur ordered nursing care only, and the administration of the drug DF118 at the discretion of the nurse, but not more than every four hours, for baby John Pearson, who had Down's syndrome. In effect this was terminal sedation, a point addressed by Helga Kuhse in her paper 'A Modern Myth. That Letting Die is not the Intentional Causation of Death: Some Reflections on the Trial and Acquittal of Dr Leonard Arthur'.[5]

Clearly choice is still involved, however, as well as intention. Michael Tooley argues that there is no difference between intentionally killing and intentionally letting die.[6] James Rachels goes even further, asserting that letting die has no defence where prolonged suffering is involved. On this view, there is no morally significant difference between killing and letting die.[7]

Rachels offers as an example two scenarios in which a wicked uncle plans to kill his baby nephew for the sake of an inheritance. In both cases, the uncle goes upstairs with the intention of drowning the child in the bath to collect the inheritance. In one scenario, he does so; in the other, the child slips under the water and falls unconscious just as he enters the room, and he stays and watches it drown. There would seem to be no morally significant difference between these two cases.

One argument against this conclusion, and in favour of the view that killing is always worse, is that an agent who kills causes death, whereas an agent who lets die merely allows nature to take its course. This seems to me highly dubious. We interfere with nature so often and in so many ways, particularly in a medical context, why not here? It seems arbitrary in the extreme to draw the line at this juncture – unless other issues are at stake.

Another argument is that drawing this distinction sets limits to our duties and responsibilities. This seems a more plausible argument. I am not as responsible for failing to aid starving African children as I would be if I had directly killed them. At first glance, this seems counter-intuitive. Sometimes we *are* held responsible for our acts of omission, as in cases of neglect.

Nor is it the case that, while we are obliged not to interfere or harm, we are not obliged to assist. This is shown to be absurd in cases like that suggested by Singer of a child drowning in a puddle. Quite simply, any onlooker *ought* to help. This case is easier, and therefore less equivocal, than a situation of someone drowning in a lake where there may be some risk to the onlooker.

There seems then to be no difference between killing and letting die in cases where both directly cause death. But if I fail to give a donation to charity to help starving children in Africa, I may be guilty of freeriding on others' altruism and of moral laziness, but cannot be said to have directly caused death.

Charlesworth offers the most defensible account of the killing/letting die distinction in the context of the developing recognition of the right of a person freely to determine and control the mode of his or her death.[8] Legislation has evolved to enable the competent patient to refuse medical treatment and so bring about his or her death. Still, in most jurisdictions, I may not actively cause the termination of my life by direct intervention – by killing myself or by asking a doctor or nurse to kill me.

Killing/letting die therefore remains in that context a valid if fine distinction. However there is growing scepticism about its use, and many cases where it seems completely artificial.

Acts/omissions

The 'acts'/'omissions' distinction is another attempt to demarcate one class of actions as less reprehensible than another, or even acceptable – in this case, failing to act. On this view, someone who refrained from acting to assist, and so brought about death, is less culpable than someone who took action and directly brought about death. This distinction may well seem one of equivocation and without substance, and not only to a consequentialist. Samaritan laws hold people culpable who fail to render assistance that does not put themselves at risk – though increasing litigiousness is working against this, by making people wary of offering assistance in case they are then later held liable for any adverse outcomes. In the case of a doctor rather than a bystander at a road accident or drowning, by virtue of role and specialist knowledge, failing to treat or to act or to stop a patient taking their own life may seem to be malpractice or negligence or poor judgement, but may seem clearly not to be as weighty a matter or as liable to moral scrutiny as actions undertaken. Is this really so?

What if the omission to warn of likely adverse outcomes of medication or treatment, for example, had major consequences? Omissions can be 'thick' and actions 'thin' or slight. And there is the problem of picking the correct (i.e. non-arbitrary) description of the action. For example, a man is moving his arm, pumping water, replenishing the water supply of the house and poisoning the inhabitants. All four descriptions depict the same behavioural movements, but each level imports a further degree of purpose and, at the last level, inadvertent effect, assuming that an unknown toxic water source is part of the background conditions.

This latent purposiveness was a problem for behaviourism, in the need to give physical descriptions of a rat's behaviour: was it seeing a stimulus as a circle or as a cue for a left turn? Was it jumping to the right or to the white card? Some reference has to be made to how the animal sees the situation, and this can only be described in mentalistic language.[9] This problem of intentionality is the mark of the mentalistic – of hoping, believing, fearing, intending – where how something is described is absolutely crucial to determining its truth value. 'Oedipus intended to kill the king' and 'Oedipus intended to kill the man on the bridge' both refer to the same man as the victim, but the first is false and the second true, given Oedipus' ignorance of the identity of the man on the bridge. ('Oedipus killed the king' and 'Oedipus killed the man on the bridge' both remain true.) Intentionality is a term used philosophically to convey the idea that people can have real hopes, beliefs and fears, even when they have no basis in the real world. The nineteenth-century philosopher and psychologist Franz Brentano regarded this as the distinctive characteristic of mental phenomena. Describe them one way and they are true; describe them another way and they are false, as we saw with the dilemma of how to characterise the rat's jumping behaviour. How do we choose the correct description? A lot may ride on this.

Foreseen but unintended effects – the 'double effects' argument

These are well known problems in the philosophy of action, but they do highlight the problem of identifying an action neutrally, without covertly smuggling in intention. Was the doctor doing A or B? Well, that depends. And here we are lead to probably the most recalcitrant and powerful distinction of all – foreseen and unintended consequences, on which turns the law of double effect.[10] What was foreseen, but a side-effect of what was directly intended, thus becomes extenuated, at least partially. For example, the directly intended effect of dropping the atom bomb on Nagasaki was to bring the Second World War to a close by bringing about the surrender of the Japanese; the foreseen but not directly intended effect was that 74,000 people were killed (the exact number was not foreseen, but that the number would be huge certainly was). On this view, those responsible were morally responsible only for what they directly intended. To take a relevant medical example, escalating doses of morphine may relieve a patient's pain; a side-effect is that they may repress the respiratory system to the point where the patient dies. Is this euthanasia? Is it killing, as opposed to letting die? It seems ordinary rather than extraordinary or heroic treatment. It is clearly an act rather than an omission. Is it palliative care? Or, if done on request, is it physician-assisted voluntary euthanasia?

What is crucial here is the doctor's intent. This argument allows more room than excusing an action on the basis that the outcome was not expected. The outcome may indeed have been expected. Using this argument, the outcome may be likely, probable or even certain. There is no need to plead ignorance or fabricate surprise. All that is necessary is to insist that the primary motive, the direct intention, was something other than to bring about the patient's death. There is a problem here with the concept of intention. Can it bear the weight it currently does? Apart from empirical problems of hypocrisy, there is the deeper philosophical problem of intentionality, which has just been outlined.

Some may see this emphasis on intention as casuistical and evasive. Yet it is an argument that still carries enormous weight. Lord Devlin (then Justice Devlin) used it in 1957 in the trial of Dr John Bodkin Adams, who had given doses of morphine and other opiates to Mrs Morrell, an elderly patient in agony. Lord Devlin directed the jury that 'a doctor is entitled to do all that is proper and necessary to relieve pain and suffering even if the measures he takes may incidentally shorten life'. This was in the context where 'the first purpose of medicine, the restoration of health, can no longer be achieved'. However, Lord Devlin concluded: 'it remains the fact, and it remains the law, that no doctor, nor any man, no more in the case of the dying than the healthy, has the right deliberately to cut the thread of human life.'[11]

Is this still so? It begs the question on the very point at issue – that the case of the dying is significantly different from that of the healthy and new options might apply.

This position seems still to be adhered to. It was the position taken by the Australian Medical Association at their May 2002 conference, which affirmed opposition to euthanasia, but endorsed the situation where the doctor's primary intent is to relieve pain, for example by escalating morphine doses, even though the foreseen concomitant is death by suppressing respiration.

The stress on intention and causation may seem fundamentally antithetical to the role of the doctor and the trust that should characterise the relation between doctor and patient. Certainly that trust can occasionally be abused, but it would seem better policy to devise safeguards against that, rather than let the mere possibility dictate the whole policy.

The Hippocratic Oath is a powerful influence here. It is often cited in a fundamentalist way, particularly the vow:

> I will neither give a deadly drug to anybody if asked for it, nor will I make a suggestion to that effect.

To cure and to care are twin imperatives of medicine, as is the duty to relieve suffering. Particularly when the patient is

requesting it, assistance with dying might be seen as an extension
of care, even though it is a direct challenge to the Hippocratic
ethic. As the Tony Bland case shows, a lethal injection is a killing
not a letting die, made conscionable in this case by quality of life
considerations.

The slippery slope

Why is the Hippocratic ethic held to so absolutely? One reason
seems to be fear of a slippery slope,[12] that it will be impossible to
hold the line and prevent extension to less justifiable situations.
The slippery slope argument is a long-standing and powerful
one in philosophy. Basically, it occurs when the argument moves
from something that may be defensible in situation A to situation B, where it seems unacceptable and even quite horrific. This
conclusion retrospectively invalidates both the principle that was
extended and the conclusion in situation B.

An example is that of neomorts (brain dead mothers, like
Marion Ploch and Trisha Marshall). Robyn Rowland[13] moves
the discussion from the dozen documented cases of brain dead
women being kept alive for the sake of the foetuses they were
carrying (in one case, at the grandparents' request; in another,
involving a dispute between the husband and the woman's lover
over ownership of the foetus) to the possibility that neomorts
could be used deliberately for surrogacy and even as egg donors.
After all, such a 'pregnancy machine' could not try to claim her
children. These possibilities are less far-fetched in the light of the
recent discussion of the possibility of using stem cells from foetuses and embryos for therapeutic cloning and even reproductive
cloning, which raises the prospect of a person being born who
had not had a living parent.

The slippery slope argument is well suited to areas where there
is a lack of consensus or determinateness – in this case about
human nature and what constitutes a person. It is usually used
in a conservative, fearful, 'holding the line' way.

In the end, the issue comes down to adherence to the Hippocratic Oath and a fear of the abyss that yawns at the bottom of
the slippery slope. Yet there is no evidence that this is so, and
the only evidence currently available – the Dutch experience of
decriminalising and later legalising euthanasia – in fact suggests
the contrary (see chapter 6).

Similarly, there is no reason why the Hippocratic Oath could not be reinterpreted or taken as a guide only. Doing otherwise will not help us think through the novel possibilities that medical and technological advances will continue to challenge us with. Past practice and tradition can be a precedent, yes, but need not chain us.

It is hard work in a liberal democracy to sort out what to make of such challenges and to achieve any kind of ethical consensus. What can be said is that these conceptual twists and turns have not succeeded in achieving clarity – or consensus. They may, in fact, have contributed to confusion as to what euthanasia actually is.

Voluntary/involuntary, active/passive euthanasia

Bioethics literature since the 1970s has drawn on two influential sets of distinctions in evaluating euthanasia, which continues the pattern of deploying binary oppositions, one of which is more acceptable. These distinctions are between voluntary and involuntary euthanasia,[14] and – alternatively or cross-cutting – active and passive euthanasia.[15] Other terms – positive and negative euthanasia – are also used, adding to the potential confusion.

Voluntary euthanasia occurs where the patient freely chooses and may ask a doctor to administer a lethal injection to hasten death. Involuntary euthanasia occurs when death is a result of actions carried out without consent, or is imposed, or where no voluntariness exists, such as with permanent vegetative state patients (though McGuire (1987)[16] suggests calling this last category non-voluntary, the two are more usually run together as involuntary).

Active euthanasia (or positive euthanasia) occurs when a deliberate act such as a lethal injection or a lethal dose of pills or omission results in the patient's death. Passive euthanasia (or negative euthanasia) occurs when death results from a deliberate omission or withholding of life-supporting care or treatment, such as antibiotics, nutrition and hydration, or mechanical life support.

These distinctions generate four possible types of euthanasia:

- Voluntary active: the doctor deliberately acts to cause death, for example by injecting a lethal dose of drugs at the patient's request.

- Voluntary passive: the doctor, at the patient's request, suspends treatment, which hastens the patient's death.
- Involuntary active: death is caused by actions taken without reference to the patient's wishes.
- Involuntary passive: death is caused by omissions or withholding of treatment carried out without reference to the patient's wishes.

In the last two cases, of course, the argument may be made that such action was taken in the patient's interest or to reduce the patient's suffering.

In descending order of moral legitimacy or supportability, one may rank voluntary active euthanasia, voluntary passive euthanasia, involuntary passive euthanasia and involuntary active euthanasia. Ho,[17] in an interesting study, investigates responses to these distinctions.

For and against euthanasia

Voluntary euthanasia, whether active or passive, is more easily defensible because of the patient's exercise of autonomy.

When the four strands are not kept clearly distinct, arguments against legalising euthanasia often turn on the perceived and feared inevitability of the slide from voluntary to non-voluntary, and further, to involuntary euthanasia. This is an argument put by those who are willing to concede there may be rare and extreme situations where voluntary euthanasia is appropriate, rather than those who argue on stricter sanctity of life grounds that voluntary euthanasia is never acceptable.

The debate, then, currently centres on the justifiability of voluntary euthanasia. (Voluntary euthanasia is defined as different from assisted suicide because, in the case of voluntary euthanasia, another person is directly involved in a way that is similar in effect to murder. Some opponents of voluntary euthanasia do equate the two.) What people are arguing about are, of course, practices rather than labels.

The arguments in favour can be summed up as based on:

- individual autonomy and the right to choose;
- loss of dignity and the right to maintain dignity;
- reduction of suffering;

- justice and the demand to be treated fairly (where assisted suicide is not an option).

The arguments against are primarily based on:

- the sanctity of life doctrine;
- the possibility of misdiagnosis and recovery (developments in brain imaging are important here);
- risk of abuse (by unscrupulous relatives or one group over another);
- non-necessity (the medical profession currently handles such cases and no legislative changes are necessary);
- discrimination (treating some lives as less worthy than others), which may be seen as a variant of sanctity of life);
- irrational or mistaken or imprudent choice (which may be guarded against in the procedures);
- the slippery slope argument.

The most powerful argument in favour, in my view, is the argument in terms of individual autonomy, as the other three can be brought in under its rubric. The two most powerful arguments against are the sanctity of life doctrine and the slippery slope.[18]

The idea that human life is sacred and inviolable, and taking it is always wrong, had to accommodate the exceptions of just war theory – killing in wartime – plus self-defence and, for some, capital punishment. It could be argued that euthanasia could be seen as another exception. If this is too hard a result to achieve, it could also be argued on liberal grounds that religion should not dictate legislation or public policy. (The bioethicist Margaret Somerville in her book *Death Talk* appeals to a notion of the 'secular sacred', which may be seen as a secular version of the sanctity of life, but this is not uncontroversial. So too does Ronald Dworkin in *Life's Dominion*.)

It is not too much of an oversimplification, then, to sum up the preceding distinctions in a nutshell and to say that the autonomy argument is the leading (that is the most commonly resorted to and commanding broadest assent) argument in support of voluntary euthanasia, and the slippery slope argument is the leading argument against.

This leaves the slippery slope argument – the fear of a theoretical and/or practical slide from voluntary euthanasia to involuntary euthanasia – as the greatest hurdle of principle and policy that confronts the legalisation of voluntary euthanasia.[19]

The debate is at once moral, political, and strategic.

At the moral level, it is an elementary dictum in ethics that 'ought implies can': I cannot be held responsible for something I have no possibility of performing. Only if I can or could have done something can it be said I ought to do, or have done, it. Conversely, in the realm of medical, scientific and technological advances over the past few decades, and into the future in as yet unforeseen ways, 'can' does not straightforwardly imply 'ought'. There are things that now *can* be done that as individuals and as a society we deem *ought* not be done, and there will be varying opinions about what these things are. To some people, and some groups in society, this may be self-evidently so, in the case of some issues – for example, cryogenics or human reproductive cloning – and these issues become very difficult to manage within the confines of a liberal democratic society. Euthanasia is an issue that is more contested, and hence even more difficult to manage in a liberal society. It was accepted in the ideal society described by Sir Thomas More in his *Utopia* (1516); for others, such as Francis Fukuyama in *The Postmodern Future*, it would be more a symptom of dystopia, of technology, producing alienation and dehumanisation. Even those who are optimistic about the potential of advances in medical and scientific technology, however, acknowledge the need for regulation and ethical assessment, so that the technological tail does not wag the human dog. How can this best be achieved in a liberal democratic society?

At the political level, what is required is a higher-order consensus of commitment to the rule of law and democratic process, to avoid turning 'hot button' issues such as abortion and euthanasia into triggers for riots, like those in the US in 1996. The rider here is J. S. Mill's warning of the 'tyranny of the majority': fifty-one per cent in favour does not make something right, or there would be no possibility of moral progress. Great leaders, from Buddha and Jesus to Gandhi and Martin Luther King, were distinguished by teachings which challenged the consensus of their times.

The above discussion, it is hoped, has contributed to clarity, even if not to consensus. That is a further step, and one that is hard enough to achieve even with the apparently more straight-forward issue of resource allocation.

Resource allocation choices

With this important rider in mind, should such consensus be achieved, even this is not enough for the way ahead to be straight. Stark choices will remain concerning resource allocation. In Australia in August 2003, for example, news of a spring-loaded implant for a six-year-old boy with cancer was greeted as a break-through. It will save him from having his leg amputated, and at six, a normal lifespan stretches ahead of him. The cost was $63,000 – paid from the public purse. The announcing doctor hastened to point out this would save $500,000 in operations over the course of his lifetime. The economic justification had to be put. It is a large amount of money to spend on one pa-tient when wards are closing, staff and funding are being cut, and waiting lists are lengthening. This was followed by news of the first triple transplant in Australia, on Jason Grey, a twenty-two year old with cystic fibrosis. Again, this is a tremendous medical breakthrough; it is also an enormous expense for one patient.

To generalise this problem and show how resource rationing is exacerbating pressures on physicians, Molloy cites[20] the number of potential recipients for heart transplants as 25,000 to 32,000 per annum, but the number of available hearts is only 1,000 to 2,000. He hypothesises that a kidney, heart, lung or liver trans-plant programme has been funded and is successful, with over 100 people on the waiting list. The seven people who top the list are:

- A seventy-year-old inventor. He is working on a new form of engine, fuelled on garbage, which may make the petrol engine obsolete. He has already developed many socially beneficial inventions.
- A sixty-five-year-old grandmother with seven sons and twenty-four grandchildren. Her son is the chief administrator of the region who controls the budget for the programme. She still cares for her youngest son, who has Down's syndrome. He will have to go into an institution if she dies.

- A forty-five-year-old designer. He has a large business employing hundreds of people. He is internationally renowned and has won many awards for his work. If he dies, all his employees will lose their jobs.
- A forty-year-old widow and mother of four children aged eleven, nine, seven and three. She works part-time and is the sole supporter of the family. Her husband was a decorated war hero.
- A twenty-five-year-old mother with two young infants.
- A fifteen-year-old high school student with an A academic average, who is the only daughter of a prominent politician.
- A six-year-old boy.

This is an excruciating ramification of some well-known anti-utilitarian dilemmas, from William Godwin's famous 1793 example of Archbishop Fenelon and his chambermaid to modern variations on this theme. Do you, for example, save your mother or Einstein, a chimpanzee or a brain-dead baby or a Picasso painting from a fire? Who should be rescued from the train track, or allowed into the lifeboat? The prospect of making such choices is, however, not a parlour game, but part of the everyday working life of physicians.

Molloy suggests arranging the seven in rank order. Then consider what you would do if you heard that the person you had picked was obese, diabetic, blind, gay, black, a Muslim (Jew, Catholic, Mormon, Hindu), had a criminal record or was paralysed from the waist down and confined to a wheelchair. He asks whether any of those factors affects your choice, and the further, challenging question – should they?

This excellent thought experiment brings out that there is increasing opprobrium for 'lifestyle' diseases. It was evident with AIDS, and is now apparent in relation to drinking, smoking and obesity. These are increasingly tending to be seen as moral failings, rather than medical conditions. It might well be argued that a lung transplant should not be 'wasted' on a recidivist smoker.

These problems will remain. The obvious reasons are that there is not enough money to make them all disappear, life expectancy is lengthening and technology is curing more people. In addition, there are increasing expectations concerning autonomy and rights.

It is easy to see why euthanasia will remain such a contentious issue, as society is faced with more and more people with a poor quality of life.

What is to be done? How can these decisions be made, ethically, transparently and democratically?[21]

Two examples of decision procedures

One famous and interesting attempt at community consultation over health care priorities occurred in the state of Oregon in 1987, when people in that state were asked to choose whether they wanted basic medical services extended to 300 disadvantaged people or continue a major organ transplant programme for thirty potential patients. The issue was decided in favour of the disadvantaged and the organ transplant programme was discontinued. The Oregon Basic Services Act was passed in 1989, setting up the Oregon Health Services Commission to determine priorities in health service and to promote community consensus on the 'social values' to be used to guide allocation decisions. A Quality of Well-Being (QWB) scale was devised to measure the value society places on various medical priorities such as prevention of death, functional disability, alleviation of pain or depression. Telephone and personal surveys were used. A ranked list of health services was produced, listing seventeen categories, which were ranked after forty-seven public meetings were held throughout Oregon. Each condition or treatment was given a cost-benefit priority. The state legislature was to consider the Commission's order of health care priorities, but not alter them – only determine how many health services could be funded, beginning from the top of the list, and then whether additional funds were necessary.

The values which emerged as priorities in the Oregon scheme were prevention, quality of life, cost-effectiveness, ability to function and equity.

The Quality of Life Years (QALY) approach has some similarities.[22] Health conditions and treatments are given a numerical weighting on the basis of objective data and interviews with a representative group of people who estimate the worth or quality of life likely to be the outcome of a given treatment. The cost of the treatment is assessed and the treatment is then given a cost-QALY rating. In the United Kingdom in 1982 it cost $800 to obtain one QALY through a heart transplant and $1,200 for one QALY by hip replacement. The QALY approach advocated by some UK health economists as a means of guiding public policy in the allocation of health care funding has some similarities to this.

The QALY approach favoured by health economists may, however, seem an over-technologised, impersonal and unsatisfactory procedure. It may also have counter-intuitive consequences, as Max Charlesworth has argued, citing a UK health economist who pointed out that it would be better, on a QALY basis, for managers with a specific sum of money to spend, to allocate it to telling people to stop smoking rather than to treating people needing hip replacements or dialysis. Such an approach may help decide between two types of procedure, but not between two patients for the same resource or procedure – which is presumably where some of the most difficult choice dilemmas lie, as Molloy's hypothetical list brought out.

Ethical values cannot be determined by majority. This shows the difficulty of operationalising, and yet the indispensability of considering, quality of life. One can see why the attempt might be made, and regard it as worthwhile, laudable. At most, however, such an approach can indicate social priorities. It may be helpful in indicating the level of support a society gives to health, and thus its community consultation/surveys/newspaper polls pecking order in the government budget. It may also be crucial in indicating the level of support, or indeed demand, for legislative change on a particular issue.

At the most macro level, in the case of resource allocation, community involvement may be direct, as in the Oregon approach, or indirect, as tacit support for a government's approach. Government organisations and professional bodies are also involved in setting out principles and guidelines, and in regulation. Individual hospitals and hospital committees are involved at the next level, and finally, individual doctors, exercising their discretion and judgement, in performing their own medical and ethical triage.

Resource allocation decisions are value-laden, in some cases covertly and in others overtly. It is, as Charlesworth has pointed out, a mistake to assume 'that if we can devise acceptable forms of cost-benefit rationing of health-care resources the ethical questions can be left to look after themselves'.[23]

Not only do ethical decisions play a part at all levels of the allocation process, but different kinds of ethical issue arise at the different levels – those that emerge at a clinical level are unlike those at the institutional or hospital level. And ethical questions present themselves in more subtle ways at the individual physician–patient level, which is where the question of euthanasia typically arises.

Euthanasia, by contrast with the macro level, seems a more private matter, between a patient and a doctor. The resources involved are slight, inexpensive and not usually the issue. Indeed, cessation of resources may be what is requested. Why should society be involved at all, one may ask, apart from society's traditional duty of care to its citizens and oversight role in monitoring births, deaths and marriages? Just as having an abortion – unlike an appendicectomy – is not an uncontroversial procedure, because it impinges on society's beliefs about life and human dignity, so does euthanasia, and runs up against society's parameters about what is permissible. Euthanasia policy and practice are ineradicably value-laden.

The individual and the state

The choices involved are not economically driven, but are between intractable incommensurables. Thus the central question is the relative role of the individual and the state. For a Millian liberal, in the context of euthanasia, the only expert, the only reliable judge of quality of life, is the agent in question.

If your life could be saved at the expense of your hearing or your sight, which would it be? People would opt differently, according to their values and interests. It is likely that most people would choose to forgo hearing, but some would not – imagine Beethoven being presented with that dilemma. It is, however, a choice for the individual concerned.

John Stuart Mill's argument on that point was unequivocal:

> The sole end for which mankind are warranted, individually or collectively, in interfering with the liberty of action of any of their number is self-protection. The only purpose for which power can be rightfully exercised over any member of a civilised society, against his will, is to prevent harm to others. His own good, either physical or moral, is not a sufficient warrant. In the part which merely

concerns himself, his independence is, of right, absolute. Over himself, over his own body and mind, the individual is sovereign.[24]

In his famous essay *On Liberty*, Mill argues strongly for a sphere of individual sovereignty:

> There is a sphere of action in which society ... has, if any, only an indirect interest; comprehending all that part of a person's life or conduct which affects only himself ... This core sphere, where the individual has sovereignty, comprises: first, consciousness, second, liberty of tastes and pursuits, of framing the plan of one's life to suit one's own character ... The only freedom which deserves the name is that of pursuing one's own good in one's own way.[25]

This is a very strong, positive, eudaimonistic or self-realisation conception of liberty, not the negative, freedom from interference conception commonly associated with Mill's name.

Mill's conception of a worthwhile human life emphasises individuality, creativity and self-determination, and he regards as distinctive human endowments the faculties of perception, discriminative feeling, mental activity and moral choice. These faculties can be developed only by the individual in a society that espouses and practises freedom in its legal, political and social institutions and practices.

The man on the bridge

For those still unconvinced that a person's own good is not a sufficient reason for interfering, Mill describes a hypothetical situation where a person is attempting to cross an unsafe bridge and there is no time to warn him of the danger he is in:

> They might seize him and turn him back, without any real infringement of his liberty; for liberty consists in doing what one desires, and he does not desire to fall into the river. Nevertheless, when there is not a certainty, but only a danger of mischief, no one but the person himself can judge of the sufficiency of the motive which may prompt him to incur the risk: in this case, therefore ... he ought, I conceive, to be only warned of the danger, not forcibly prevented from exposing himself to it.[26]

On this view, the bystander is justified only in alerting him to the condition of the bridge – that is, supplying him with information, pointing out risk. Anything more is interference and paternalistic. This shows how far Mill will go to defend individual sovereignty, where paternalistic, moralistic or welfarist reasons for intervention do not apply. This is the area of what he calls self-regarding actions, which include first the inward domain of consciousness and second, liberty of tastes and pursuits, and framing of a plan of one's life to suit one's own character. Mill insists, in what has become a familiar formula, that an individual ought to be left to do what he or she likes when his or her conduct affects only himself or herself and other individuals only with their free, undeceived consent. Only the unfavourable judgement of others, not punishment, is appropriate in this area and it is inappropriate to enforce or prevent what is properly self-regarding:

> Neither one person nor any number of persons is warranted in saying to another human creature of ripe years, that he should not do with his life for his own benefit what he chooses to do with it. He is the person most interested in his own well-being ... With respect to his own feelings and circumstances, the most ordinary man or woman has means of knowledge immeasurably surpassing those that can be possessed by anyone else. In this department, therefore, of human affairs, individuality has its proper field of action.[27]

This is a quote that resonates in relation to euthanasia. So too does the following question:

> What the agent is free to do, ought other persons to be equally free to counsel or instigate?[28]

This question, so clearly relevant in the case of assisted suicide (though this is not the context in which Mill poses it), is answered unequivocally:

> Whatever it is permitted to do, it must be permitted to advise to do.[29]

Mill qualifies this only when the instigator derives a personal benefit from his advice.

His defence of freedom in the area of self-regarding actions thus rests on his insistence that the individual must be a source of his or her own ends. For Mill it is axiomatic that a life cannot be a good life unless it is freely chosen.

Mill's primary focus is the individual subject of classical liberalism. He shows how choice is central to the development of the person, and to the parallel between the progressive individual and the progressive liberal democratic state. Both require the fostering of choice, diversity of tastes and environments, and experiments in living. It is quite a radical individualism. Mill is wary of infringement by the state, but equally of infringement by the majority. This comes out in what he says about truth and the importance of maverick opinion, in his assertion that silencing of discussion is an assumption of infallibility, as well as in his constant criticism of prejudice and custom as deadening factors that bring a progressive society to a halt.

Mill's emphasis is on individual freedom – as much civil and social liberty as possible – and his political argument is that a good state maximises and respects individual choice. At the level of the individual, choice is quite clearly constitutive of the individual. It is therefore the key to both individual liberty and social progress. 'My choice' is not just a consumerist notion; it is much deeper, integral to and constitutive of a person, and thus its violation is serious.

Moreover, for Mill, human nature is not a given, but a creation. He argues against the 'favourable prejudgement' associated with the word 'nature', pointing out that nature is ethically neutral – as destructive as it is benign – and hence no basis for prescription. This argument is important to keep in mind in the context of euthanasia, where frequent appeals are made to 'let nature take its course'. Moreover, the very question 'What is natural?' cannot yield a shortcut decision procedure, for the answer to that too is ever changing – knives? spectacles? antibiotics? ventilators? – and a variable matter of choice.

Given Mill's emphasis on the self-regarding sphere and on individuality, it is an individual like this who is deserving of human dignity and who exercises moral autonomy. Mill's is a secular account, which delineates the relative spheres and proper prerogatives of individual and state.

Since euthanasia offers a perfect example which fulfils Mill's conditions for individual sovereignty, this raises the question of how end-of-life issues might best be handled in a liberal society.

A liberal society

A liberal society is based on the principle of personal liberty: to the greatest degree possible, people should be free to make their own life-choices and decisions. The state, acting through the law, should opt out as far as possible of the preserve of personal morality. Paternalistic action by the state should be minimised. A strict line between the two spheres of personal morality and state intervention should be maintained. Equally importantly, in a liberal society there should be no state-imposed morality or religion.

Yet in many ethical and bioethical issues, a gap yawns between liberal ideals and existing discussion and practice, and toleration of ethical pluralism is curbed on behalf of social unity and cohesion.

What might be called pluri-culturalism is central to a liberal society, for, as Mill stressed, a liberal society not only tolerates a wide diversity of experiments in living, but encourages such diversity as a reflection and a condition of social and cultural vitality. Charlesworth takes a similar view in arguing that 'the liberal ideal provides the only real basis for a genuinely multicultural society' rather than an 'authoritarian society based upon a unitary socio-moral consensus'.

> It is a liberal act of faith that it is possible to have a society without consensus upon a substantive set of moral, religious and social values, save for consensus upon the values of personal autonomy and liberty.[30]

This excludes any attempt to impose 'a particular consensus based upon a partisan or sectional set of moral or social values'. Sub-groups may espouse their own religious or moral positions, but cannot demand that they be imposed upon the whole community. This is absolutely central to a liberal society.

A liberal society is thus a very devolved almost procedural, concept stressing individual self-determination at its core.

A good example of how such a liberal approach might play out on a particular issue is exemplified in the UK by the hugely influential Wolfenden Report (1957).[31] Clearly influenced by Mill, the Report adopted a sophisticated approach to the decriminalisation of prostitution and homosexuality between consenting adults. In very Millian language, it held that it is 'not the function of the law to intervene in the private lives of citizens' and that 'there must remain a realm of private morality and immorality which is, in brief and crude terms, not the law's business'.

Crucially, by decriminalising prostitution, homosexuality or abortion, the state is not approving of them; it is simply declaring that these acts are outside the ambit of public morality, and are out of bounds for state intervention and the criminal law.

This might be a precedent for the most enlightened approach to adopt to euthanasia, particularly as it does not preclude some degree of state regulation, though not via the criminal law.

Part Two will consider the approach taken to euthanasia in four countries – how the debate evolved, what emphases were significant and how the issue was managed in countries with different political systems and approaches to regulation. After the fairly theoretical nature of the two chapters that constitute Part One, it is appropriate that the four chapters that comprise Part Two focus in some detail on the people whose courageous stands and tragic stories have driven what progress there has been in relation to euthanasia.

It is to be hoped that the need for such repetitious and contested stories will diminish in the future, as voluntary euthanasia and assisted suicide become normalised and accommodated within a truly liberal democratic society.

Notes

1. Gardner: *re BWV*, VSC 173, 29 May 2003.
2. M. Somerville, *Death Talk* (Montreal: McGill-Queens University Press, 2001).
3. W. Molloy, *Vital Choices* (Harmondsworth: Penguin, 1994).
4. H. Kuhse, 'Euthanasia', in *A Companion to Ethics*, ed. P. Singer (Oxford: Blackwell, 1993), p. 298.
5. Helga Kuhse, 'A Modern Myth. That Letting Die is not the Intentional Causation of Death: Some Reflections on the Trial and Acquittal of Dr Leonard Arthur', *Journal of Applied Philosophy* 1, No. 1 (1984).

6. In M. J. Johnstone, *Bioethics: A Nursing Perspective* (Sydney: W. B. Saunders/Baillière Tindall, 1989), p. 261.
7. Ibid.
8. M. Charlesworth, *Bioethics in a Liberal Society* (Cambridge: Cambridge University Press, 1993), p. 34.
9. G. Tulloch, 'Skinner and Seeing Red' (Unpublished MA, University of Melbourne, 1980).
10. A. B. Shaw, 'Two Challenges to the Double Effect Doctrine: Euthanasia and Abortion', *Journal of Medical Ethics* Vol. 28 (2002); A. R. Derse, 'Is There a Lingua Franca for Bioethics at the End of Life?', *Journal of Law, Medicine and Ethics* Vol. 28, No. 3 (2000).
11. P. Devlin, *The Enforcement of Morals* (Oxford: Oxford University Press, 1968).
12. G. Tulloch, 'Avoiding the Slippery Slope in Ethics and Bioethics', *Nursing Inquiry* Vol. 3 (1996).
13. R. Rowland, *Living Laboratories* (Sydney: Sun, 1992).
14. N. Campbell, 'A Problem; for the Idea of Voluntary Euthanasia', *Journal of Medical Ethics* Vol. 25, No. 3 (1999); T. McConnell, 'On an Alleged Problem for Voluntary Euthanasia', *Journal of Medical Ethics* Vol. 26, No. 3 (2000).
15. Sklansky, 'Neonatal Euthanasia: Moral Considerations and Criminal Liability'; J. P. Moreland, 'James Rachels and the Active Euthanasia Debate', *JETS* 31/1 (1988).
16. Johnstone, *Bioethics*.
17. R. Ho, 'Assessing Attitudes Towards Euthanasia: An Analysis of the Subcategorical Approach to Right to Die Issues', *Personality and Individual Differences* Vol. 25 (1998).
18. W. Wright, 'Historical Analogies, Slippery Slopes and the Question of Euthanasia', *Journal of Law, Medicine and Ethics* Vol. 28, No. 2 (2000).
19. Richard Ashcroft, 'Euthanasia, Regulation and Slippery Slopes', *Palliative Medicine* Vol. 17 (2003).
20. Molloy, *Vital Choices*, p. 65.
21. Charlesworth, *Bioethics in a Liberal Society*.
22. H. Caton, 'The Resource Allocation Dilemma', *Health Cover* Vol. 2, No. 4 (1993); Charlesworth, *Bioethics in a Liberal Society*.
23. Charlesworth, *Bioethics in a Liberal Society*, p. 110.
24. J. S. Mill, *Three Essays* (Oxford: Oxford University Press, 1978), p. 233.
25. Ibid., p. 226.
26. Ibid p. 118.
27. J. S. Mill, *Collected Works*, Vol. XVIII, p. 277.
28. Mill, *Three Essays*, p. 120.
29. Ibid., p. 121.
30. Charlesworth, *Bioethics in a Liberal Society*.
31. *Report of the Committee on Homosexual offences and Prostitution.* London: HMSO, 1957.

Part Two

3

Death and Dying in America

It is appropriate that America is the first country to be considered in Part Two, as bioethics really began as a field there more than thirty years ago, when the Hastings Center was set up to consider the human meaning of medical developments. Death and dying were among its original four areas of concern (the others being behaviour control; genetic screening, counselling and engineering; and population policy and family planning), and concern first manifested over issues to do with termination of treatment and letting die – issues revolving round choice and death.

It was America too that was the source of the influential brain death criterion that became the standard definition of death internationally (with the exception of Japan), after the 1968 Harvard Ad Hoc Committee.

Chapter 2 discussed the organ donation context for the establishment of the Harvard Committee. It was this that prompted the pressure to move to a more specialised criterion of cortical death. The two key cases mentioned were American: Karen Quinlan (1975), which turned on whether artificial respiration should be ceased; and Nancy Cruzan (1983), which turned on whether nutrition and hydration could be withdrawn. These cases provide the background to events described in the present chapter.

America has a federal system of government, with individual states being responsible for health. However, as both the Quinlan and Cruzan cases demonstrate, troublesome cases can be appealed to the Supreme Court, and Supreme Court decisions become precedents. The federal government can also establish universal authority by legislation such as the Patient Self-Determination Act of 1990,[1] which enforced compliance in all hospitals that receive federal funding. Reports from the President's Bioethics Commission, set up in 1987 by President Reagan, are also influential.

It is a truism that hard cases make bad law. It is also apparent that advances in medicine and science will continue to produce hard cases that call for rulings. The challenge is to get ahead of the ad hoc, piecemeal approach generated by legislative responses to individual hard cases, to a proactive standpoint that anticipates and accommodates future developments. I want now to give detailed consideration to such an approach.

The Philosophers' Brief

The Philosophers' Brief on Assisted Suicide of 1997 is an excellent example[2] of argument that transcends the specific circumstances of the cases that generated it. It was written by six eminent American moral philosophers – Ronald Dworkin, Thomas Nagel, Robert Nozick, John Rawls, Thomas Scanlon, Judith Jarvis Thompson – and filed as an amicus curiae brief in two cases posing the question of whether dying patients have a right to choose death rather than continued pain and suffering. The two cases were the *State of Washington et al.* v. *Glucksberg et al.*, and *Vacco et al. v. Quill et al.*, argued 8 January 1997.

In the context where the laws of all but one American state (Oregon) forbid doctors to prescribe lethal pills for patients who want to kill themselves, groups of dying patients and their doctors in Washington State and New York sued, asking that these prohibitions be declared unconstitutional. Two federal Circuit Courts of Appeal, in Washington and New York, agreed with the plaintiffs, and Washington State and New York appealed these decisions to the Supreme Court. Sixty amicus curiae briefs were filed, including ones from the American Medical Association and the Unites States Catholic Conference. The justices' comments during oral argument indicated that the Court would reverse the decision, as they cited two versions of the 'slippery slope' argument – that it would be impossible to limit a right to assisted suicide in an acceptable way, once that right was granted.

The theoretical version of the argument denies that any principled line can be drawn between cases where assisted suicide is appropriate and where it is not. The Circuit Court recognised only a right for competent patients dying in pain to have pills prescribed that they could take themselves. This paradigm case was acceptable. Several justices queried on what grounds the right could be so limited. What of patients who are paralysed or too feeble to take pills and who request a doctor's assistance by injecting them? What too of non-terminal patients who face years of physical or emotional pain, or crippling, paralysing dependence or the foreseeable ravages of a progressive disease? And how could it be denied to anyone who had formed a settled desire to die – for example, a sixteen-year-old boy suffering unrequited love?

The last example is the one that gives me most trouble. For I want to restrain that sixteen-year-old, but it is hard to do so without being ageist ('too young'), patronising ('not had enough experience') or paternalistic ('will think better of it').

The Philosophers' Brief began by defining a very general moral and constitutional (and Millian) principle – that every competent person has the right to make momentous personal decisions which involve fundamental religious or philosophical convictions about life's value for themselves. Secondly, this principle recognises that people may make such decisions impulsively or out of emotional depression, when their act does not reflect their enduring convictions, and therefore allows that in some circumstances the state has the constitutional power to override the right, to protect citizens from mistaken and irrevocable acts of self-destruction, however paternalistic this may seem. This would justify a state's protecting an anguished adolescent, but not forcing a competent dying patient to live in agony a few weeks longer.

The second, practical version of the slippery slope argument is more complex. If assisted suicide were permitted in principle, each state would adopt regulations to ensure that a patient's decision is informed, competent and free. But some fear those regulations could not be adequately enforced and that some vulnerable patients might be pressured. The counter-argument is that such patients would be better protected. It is experience that would decide here.

The philosophers described as 'one of the great scandals of contemporary medical practice' the current two-tier system – a chosen death and an end of pain outside the law for those with connections, and stony refusals for most other people. This is a very powerful argument against the status quo, which is full of embedded hypocrisy and covert subterfuge. The philosophers quoted studies in Washington, Michigan and San Francisco of doctors helping people die in rates equalling those of The Netherlands, where assisted suicide is in effect legal, provided certain guidelines are followed.

The philosophers argued that a benefit of legalising assisted suicide might be better care while patients live, as the medical experts cited disagreed about the percentage of terminal cases in which pain can be made tolerable by palliative techniques, but they agreed that many patients did not receive the relief that could have been available to them. The factors cited include medical ignorance, fear of liability, inadequate hospital funding and failure of insurers and health care programmes to cover the cost of hospice care.

This is a central point. If most patients have no reason to fear present or future pain, one of the major motives for euthanasia and requests for assisted suicide may be diminished – diminished, not eliminated. To admit this is not, however, to say that there might not be other justifying reasons.

Adequate pain relief, however, should surely be the norm. The brief quotes the guidelines published by a network of ethics committees in the Bay Area of California, which provide, among other stringent safeguards, that a primary health care physician who receives a request for assisted suicide must make an initial referral to a hospice programme or to a physician experienced in palliative care. As the Coalition of Hospice Professionals said in their own amicus brief, 'regulation of physician assisted suicide would mandate that all palliative measures be exhausted as a condition precedent to assisted suicide'.

The philosophers found neither version of the slippery slope argument – the first, theoretical, the second, practical – very strong, but added that the Court was in a difficult position. Declaring that terminally ill patients do not have the right to control their own deaths seems alien to the constitution, as even the Solicitor General argued, and would undermine past decisions of the Court, including its position in Casey (1993), in which the Supreme Court reaffirmed the right to abortion and suggested that matters

> [i]nvolving the most intimate and personal choices a person may make in a lifetime, choices central to personal dignity and autonomy, are central to the liberty protected by the Fourteenth Amendment.

At the heart of the liberty is the right to define one's own concept of existence, of meaning, of the universe, and of the mystery of human life.[3]

Federal District Judge Rothstein of the Washington trial court applied this 'highly instructive' reasoning to end of life:

Like the abortion decision, the decision of a terminally ill person to end his or her own life involves the most intimate and personal choices a person may make in a lifetime and constitutes a choice central to personal dignity and autonomy.[4]

The philosophers argue that protecting the abortion rulings was presumably one of the aims of the Clinton administration in arguing, through the Solicitor General, for the second strategy.

Since the Cruzan decision, discussed in the brief, lawyers have generally assumed the Court would protect the right of any competent patient to have life-sustaining equipment removed from his body, even though he would then die. Judge Rothstein posed the question whether there is 'a difference for purposes of finding a Fourteenth Amendment liberty interest between refusal of unwanted treatment which will result in death and committing physician-assisted suicide in the final stages of life'. He concluded that there is not, because both are 'profoundly personal' and 'at the heart of personal liberty'.

Several justices in the oral argument invoked the 'common-sense' distinction between acts and omissions, which would justify a constitutional distinction between prescribing lethal pills and removing life support, for the latter is only a matter of 'letting nature take its course', while prescribing pills is an active intervention that brings death sooner than natural processes would.

The philosophers insist that these suggestions misunderstand the 'common-sense' distinction, which is not between acts and omissions, but between acts or omissions designed to cause death, and those that are not. This cannot justify a constitutional distinction between assisting in suicide and terminating life support. Many doctors who terminate life support do aim at death, as do those who withhold nutrition during terminal sedation.

The Supreme Court also rejected the act-omission distinction, stating that

Cruzan, by recognising a liberty interest that involves the refusal of artificial provision of life-sustaining food and water, necessarily recognises a liberty interest in hastening one's own death.[5]

Judge Reinhardt, who wrote the majority opinion, admitted that approving an assisted suicide right would necessarily lead to approving a right to euthanasia, though that must be 'answered directly in future cases, and not in this one':

We would be less than candid, however, if we did not acknowledge that for present purposes we view the critical line in right-to-die cases as the one between voluntary and involuntary termination of an individual's life.[6]

The second strategy is equally problematic – conceding a general right to assisted suicide, but allowing states to judge the risks of allowing any exercise of that right are too great. It would be dangerous for the Court to allow a state to claim a constitutional right on the grounds that the state lacks the will or resources to enforce safeguards. Moreover, it was because bills had been introduced to legalise assisted suicide or euthanasia in state legislatures – including Alaska, Arizona, Colorado, Connecticut, Hawaii, Iowa, Maine, Maryland, Massachusetts, Michigan, Nebraska, New Hampshire, New Mexico, Rhode Island and Vermont – since 1992, and all had failed, that euthanasia proponents had turned to the courts in Washington state and New York state, seeking to have laws against assisted suicide found unconstitutional.

Richard Hull pulled no punches in expressing his disapproval:

States like New York that have turned back such initiatives must bear the shame of having imposed religious majorities' philosophies on all who suffer.[7]

Lower court rulings varied, from one federal district court finding a constitutional right to assisted suicide to another denying it, with appellate courts of review producing 'even more fractured opinions' (Gorsuch). It was no wonder that both cases ended in the Supreme Court, and that the Philosophers' Brief appeared in as accessible a site as *The New York Review of Books*.

The Brief conceded that 'a state has a right to take alternative reasonable measures to insure that a patient who requested such assistance has made an informed, competent, stable and uncoerced decision', to establish procedure and even to err on the side of caution. It continues forcefully:

> But they may not use the bare possibility of error as justification for refusing to establish any procedures at all and relying instead on a flat prohibition.[8]

The Brief affirms the very Millian conclusion that

> Each individual has a right to make the 'most intimate and personal choices central to personal dignity and autonomy'. That right encompasses the right to exercise some control over the time and manner of one's death.[9]

The Philosophers' Brief is recognisably American in that it argues in terms of liberty and justice and the American constitutional tradition. In the Introduction, for example:

> Individuals have a constitutionally protected interest in making those grave judgements for themselves free from the imposition of any religious or political orthodoxy by court or legislature ... Denying the opportunity to terminally ill patients could only be justified on the basis of a religious or ethical conviction about the meaning of life itself. Our constitution forbids government to impose such convictions on its citizens.[10]

A country without a constitution could use similar arguments in terms of liberty and justice, then invoke this as precedent, and also stress the liberal principle central to democracy of 'freedom from the imposition of any religious or philosophical orthodoxy by the legislature'.

These arguments have universal resonance in liberal democratic societies. Stripped as far as possible of rights talk, they are cast in terms of principle – the principle being respect for persons. The concept of person is then cashed in Millian terms, emphasising individuality, choice and self-determination.

These are the characteristics that constitute human flourishing, and both ground and constitute a human quality of life. This, so spelt out, can serve as an ethical and clinical criterion to guide policy and practice. There are recognisable and rich affinities with Maslow's hierarchy of needs,[11] and with Nussbaum's human capabilities approach, articulated in 'Women and Human Development: The Capabilities Approach'(2000)[12] and, with Jonathan Glover, 'Women, Culture and Development'(2001),[13] which fuses an Aristotelian, eudaimonistic, self-realisation approach (which has much in common with Mill) and an approach based on the Universal Declaration of Human Rights. These capabilities are precursors to, and preconditions of, human flourishing.

This standpoint, like Maslow's hierarchy of needs, may lead to advocacy of very similar positions in practice in particular cases, and is preferable, in my view, to arguments cast in terms of the right to die.

The right to die

Jeremy Bentham famously dismissed rights rather glibly as 'nonsense on stilts'. Mill did not endorse Bentham's view – on this point he deviated significantly from him – but it is noteworthy that he cast his arguments in terms of liberty and individuality.

One problem with rights talk is that it is empty without corresponding talk of responsibilities. Who can this right be sheeted home to in the putative case of a right to die? It is in one sense empty in that, as discussed in chapter 2, it is the human condition to die. Asserted in the context of a call for euthanasia or assisted suicide, it is a call to be let die, or helped to die, now. In my view, it is as unsatisfactory and obscurantist a slogan as the right to life, and should be eschewed for similar reasons. It hijacks the debate and takes it down an inevitable dead end. The debate in America seems stuck there because so much of the argument proceeds by attempting to derive a right to die from the American Constitution.

Yet ironically, as Kass points out,[14] rights-based thinking originated with Thomas Hobbes and John Locke, and all the rights of mankind, deriving from nature, presuppose a self-interested attachment to our own lives. My private right to life or to self-preservation is asserted against tyrants or enemies, and it was to secure this right, according to Hobbes, that individuals were prepared to concede power to a Leviathan or all-powerful ruler – the alternative being a state of nature that is anarchy, or, in

Hobbes' famous phrase, life that is 'solitary, poor, nasty, brutish and short'. The liberal state was actually established to protect life.

Locke expressly rejected a natural right to suicide, distinguishing liberty from licence in a way that was later adopted by Mill (and in modern times, by A. S. Neill, the founder of Summerhill progressive school):

> Though this be a state of liberty, yet it is not a state of licence: though man in that state has an uncontrollable liberty to dispose of his person or possessions, yet he has not liberty to destroy himself.[15]

Locke is frequently held to base his view on property on a principle of self-ownership, which could then be used to justify self-destruction, since I own my body and hence my life.

> Every man has a property in his own person; this nobody has a right to but himself. The labour of his body and the work of his hands is properly his.[16]

But this 'property in his own person' is more of a political statement, one that denies ownership by any other. This property is inalienable and cannot be transferred by selling oneself into slavery. This prospect was anathema to Mill too, on the slightly different ground that it violates one's freedom to alienate one's freedom.

Immanuel Kant, who based rights in reason rather than in nature, viewed the self-willed act of self-destruction as self-contradictory:

> It seems absurd that a man can injure himself. (Injury cannot happen to one who is willing.) The Stoic considered it a prerogative of his personality as a wise man to walk out of his life with an undisturbed mind whenever he liked (as out of a smoke-filled room) not because he was afflicted by actual or anticipated ills, but simply because he could make use of nothing more in this life. ... To dispose of oneself as a mere means to some end of one's own liking is to degrade the humanity in one's person.[17]

This would certainly not endorse a 'tired of life' claim to euthanasia or assisted suicide, as in the 1986 Brongersma case in The Netherlands[18] (see chapter 6).

A right to become dead or to be made dead cannot be established on classical liberal grounds. This whole discussion occurs only in Western liberal societies, for it is only in Western liberal societies that the rights of individuals have such primacy and that there exists high-tech medicine capable of keeping people from dying in the way they may wish.

However, in America, rights-based claims have proliferated to the point where a putative right to be born has been joined by a putative right not to have been born. Rights in America are defined largely by law, especially constitutional law. Yet, as Kass also points out, the framers of the American Constitution understood rights and the role of government in a Lockean way, so there is no constitutional textual basis or support for a legal right to die.

Yet we have seen that the Supreme Court has twice issued opinions in 'right to die' cases – in 1990, in Cruzan, voting 5 to 4 in favour of the state and against the 'right to die', and in 1997 in favour of the state in the two companion cases *Washington* v. *Glucksberg* and *Vacco* v. *Quill*, which were the occasion for the Philosophers' Brief. In neither case, however, did the court categorically reject the asserted right, and Justice O'Connor expressly left room for a stronger case to emerge later – in Kass's words left 'wiggle room'. She was one of the 5 to 4 majority who included Rehnquist, Scalia, Kennedy and the then recently appointed and controversial Clarence Thomas. She filed a separate statement with Justices Ginsberg and Breyer, and made it clear that in voting with the majority, she relied on the availability of terminal sedation.[19] McStay brings out the significance of this point quite unequivocally:

> In 1997, the U.S. Supreme Court tacitly endorsed terminal sedation as an alternative to physician-assisted suicide, thus intensifying a debate in the legal and medical communities as to the propriety of terminal sedation and setting the stage for a new battleground in the 'right to die' controversy.[20]

The upshot of the parallel Glucksberg and Quill cases was thus to return the assisted suicide and euthanasia issues to the states and the political process. Justice Stevens foreshadowed a lengthy battle, analogous to the fight over capital punishment. It is a reasonable, in fact strong, empirical bet, however, that no 'right to die' case will go to the Supreme Court in the near or foreseeable future (with the proviso, depending on the result of the 2004 presidential election).

Kass analyses rights as a kind of liberty – a blameless liberty, according to Hobbes. I may not have a right to do everything I am free to do, legally or morally. Rights were political creations, fundamental to liberal politics, and initially represented negative rights against interference with our liberties. Economic, social and cultural rights were what Somerville has called second-generation rights,[21] with collective rights to development, humanitarian assistance, information and environmental well-being grafted on as a third generation of human rights. What is clearly needed is a positive-content human right that establishes at some fundamental level the right of access to at least a minimal standard of health care. Bioethics represents a specialised area of human rights in medicine, traditionally taken to be the rights to autonomy, self-determination, non-maleficence ('do no harm'), beneficence ('do good') and justice. As Sharma has pointed out,[22] these guiding principles are less concerned with consequences; medical ethics was generally considered 'a deontologic enterprise'. It is not surprising, then, that it is critiqued by consequentialists (particularly utilitarians), feminists and situationists alike.

Legal milestones

As we saw in chapter 2, the first major milestone in America was the 1968 Harvard Medical School redefinition of death to include the cessation of brain function as well as heart- and-lung function. But in 1967, Attorney Louis Kutner had drafted the first living will, and wrote a paper on it for the *Indiana Law Journal*.[23] In 1989 Elisabeth Kübler-Ross wrote her groundbreaking work *On Death and Dying*. The two together set the scene for change. By 1990, the American Voluntary Euthanasia Society had distributed 60,000 living wills modelled on Kutner's draft, and in 1993 the American Hospice Association drafted a Patient Bill of Rights, covering informed consent and the right to refuse treatment – both longstanding bioethical concerns from the 1970s.

The Quinlan case dramatically changed public opinion, due to the extensive media coverage it received. Karen Quinlan was a twenty-one-year-old who fell into a persistent vegetative state after twice stopping breathing and being resuscitated after consuming drugs and drinks at a party. Her parents were Roman Catholics and may be presumed to have views about the sanctity of life, but did not support 'extraordinary means' − a respirator and artificial nutrition via a nasogastric tube − to save life.

In March 1976 the New Jersey Supreme Court found in the Quinlans' favour. They asked that the support machine be discontinued, but nutrition continued and nature be left to take its course. The hospital first agreed, then changed its mind, citing lack of a medical precedent. The Quinlans had her father appointed his daughter's legal guardian.

California passed its Natural Death Act in the same year, giving legal status to living wills and protecting doctors from being sued for failing to treat incurable illness.

In 1980 Derek Humphry (the English journalist who wrote *Jean's Way*, an account of his wife's death from breast cancer in 1978, and who had moved to Los Angeles) founded the Hemlock Society in California (named for the Greek philosopher Socrates, who famously ended his life by taking hemlock). In 1981 he published *Let Me Die Before I Wake*, a guide to suicide, and in 1982 the eminent author Arthur Koestler and his wife committed suicide together (he was terminally ill). All these events affected public opinion. Several terminally ill people took to court requests to discontinue life-saving treatment or to refuse food and water.

In 1989 the Supreme Court considered whether the American Constitution guaranteed the right to have life-sustaining treatment withheld or withdrawn in the Nancy Cruzan case (see chapter 3). Nancy Cruzan had lost control of her car in 1983 at the age of twenty-five. She was thrown into a water-filled ditch and had stopped breathing for twenty minutes before being revived. She was in a permanent vegetative state, but because her brain stem was intact, could live indefinitely without a respirator, if given artificial nutrition and hydration. The action sought here was thus more radical than in the Karen Quinlan case, as the Cruzans sought to have her feeding tubes removed. They took their case to the Supreme Court − the first time for such a case. The Supreme Court recognised that competent adults had a constitutionally protected liberty interest that included a right to refuse medical treatment. This set a precedent, but upheld Missouri's right to insist on clear evidence that Cruzan would have exercised the right if she could. After hearing friends' testimony, the Missouri court relented and Cruzan finally died eight years after the accident. As already cited in chapter 2, her sad gravestone bore three dates:

> Born 20 July 1957
> Departed 11 Jan 1983
> At Peace 26 Dec 1990

The Quinlan and Cruzan cases have shown that advances were made at the cost of much anguish for the families involved in these groundbreaking cases. The youth of both patients added to the poignancy of their situation. Few people could fail to be moved, or fail to put themselves in the shoes of the families involved. The impact is indicated by the fact that the Society for the Right to Die received 400,000 requests for living wills following the Cruzan court ruling.[24]

In 1990 the American Medical Association adopted the position that, given an advance directive, a physician may withhold or withdraw treatment from a patient who is close to death, and may discontinue life support from a patient in a persistent vegetative state. It remains opposed to assisted suicide and voluntary euthanasia.

In 1990, too, the euthanasia and assisted suicide advocate Dr Jack Kevorkian admitted having helped a woman with Alzheimer's disease to die, and Congress passed the Patient Self-Determination Act, requiring hospitals which received federal funds to notify patients that they have a right to demand or refuse treatment. A citizen-initiated referendum on assisted suicide was filed in Washington state, and narrowly defeated.

In 1991 another doctor, Timothy Quill, published an article in the *New England Journal of Medicine*,[25] describing how he gave lethal drugs to a leukaemia patient who wanted to die. Derek Humphry's *Final Exit* gave even more explicit advice, and became a bestseller.

In 1994, a majority of delegates to a California Bar conference voted in favour of physician-assisted suicide for competent, terminally-ill patients, and Washington state's suicide law was overturned. Judge Rothstein found that outlawing assisted suicide violated the Fourteenth Amendment, and importantly concluded:

> The court does not believe that a distinction can be drawn between refusing life-sustaining medical treatment and physician-assisted suicide by an uncoerced, mentally competent, terminally ill adult.[26]

Dr Quill then filed a suit in New York to challenge the state's law against assisted suicide – one of the two cases that were the context for the Philosophers' Brief. Dr Kevorkian had been challenging the authorities ever since he built a suicide machine in the late 1980s and a woman admitted using it in 1990. He admitted having helped more than 130 people to die and was charged four times in various jurisdictions, being acquitted three times and having the other case declared a mis-trial – an indication of public sympathy. In 1998 he overstepped the mark by giving a fatal injection to a patient suffering Lou Gehrig's disease (a motor neurone disease) and sending a video of the event to CNN's 'Sixty Minutes' programme, which broadcast it. A blind eye could no longer be turned.

In 1999, Kevorkian was arrested, charged and sentenced to 10–25 years by a Michigan court. He thus became the first American doctor to be convicted of murder for helping a patient die. He continues to campaign from prison, and will be eligible for parole in 2007. His notoriety has been a mixed blessing for the cause. Glick and Hutchinson argue, however, that his assisted suicides 'provided major focusing events' and helped the rise of physician-assisted suicide on the national political agenda, based on its status as a morality policy.[27]

The Oregon Death with Dignity Act

In 1994 Oregon's Death with Dignity Act, permitting assisted suicide, was approved by voters, but did not go into effect until 1997, due to an injunction from the District Court. Importantly, the Act was passed not by the Oregon state legislature, but by the direct vote of the populace. The margin was narrow – fifty-one per cent. This was after similar initiatives had failed by bare majorities in California in 1988 (fifty-two per cent) and Washington state in 1991 (fifty-four per cent). Glick argues that these three states are liberal on personal freedom and individual rights, and religious organisations, including the Catholic church, are less powerful there than in many other states. Also, the Hemlock Society is located in California and Oregon. The narrow passage may well have been because the state medical society did not adopt a clear position on the issue. Paul bears this out, showing that rank-and-file doctors are more permissive on the issue than doctors affiliated with the AMA.[28] Significantly, the refusal in 1997 to repeal the 1994 law was carried by a stronger majority – sixty per cent.

One may be tempted to ask 'What is it about Oregon?' given its earlier initiative in adopting a Medicaid rationing plan that assigned a priority to each of hundreds of different medical treatments (see chapter 3), and the recent initiative Measure 23 or 'Health Care for All',[29] which moved close to providing an all-expenses paid, 'universal' health care coverage for all residents. This is a fascinating question which deserves to be answered, but is too far afield of the present purpose of this book.

What can be said is that Oregon is the current touchstone for the legal status of physician-assisted suicide in America, being the only state that allows it under specific guidelines. (Hawaii is currently considering a similar law.)

The Oregon Act defines physician-assisted suicide as a death caused by ingesting a lethal dose of medication obtained by prescription from a physician for the purpose of ending one's life. By contrast, euthanasia refers to death that occurs as a result of more direct intervention. The Act follows the model and the means of physician-assisted suicide advocated by Dr Timothy Quill in his 1991 *New England Journal of Medicine* article.[30]

The Act was detailed, and set four strict preconditions. A patient had to be: aged eighteen or over; a resident of the state; capable of making and communicating a clear decision; and terminally ill, with a prognosis of under six months to live. Importantly, as in The Netherlands and unlike Switzerland, Oregon has a 'residents only' provision.

The patient then has to go through the following rigorous steps:

• Make two verbal requests to the physician, at least fifteen days apart.
• Make a written request to the physician.

- The patient's physician should call in a second physician to confirm the diagnosis and progress, and the competence of the patient to make the request: any sign of depression meant the patient must be referred for counselling.
- The patient's physician should inform the patient of alternatives, such as pain management and palliative care.
- The physician should request that the patient notify his next of kin of the request.

In what seems an excellent model, the permission was thus stringently curtailed and could in no way justify 'slippery slope' alarmism. In the event, the stampede envisaged by some has not eventuated. In 1999–2003, 146 prescriptions were written, and ninety-one used. In 2001, forty-four were written and nineteen used. This evidence is important in a situation where there are so few regimes that permit assisted suicide and can therefore provide empirical evidence to rebut or support 'slippery slope' alarmists. The statute requires that individuals who request a lethal prescription be advised of alternatives to physician-assisted suicide, such as comfort care, hospice care and pain control. This contrasts markedly with the vulnerability of Kevorkian's euthanasia patients, who lacked the protection of clinical safeguards such as those in place in Oregon.[31]

In 2001, Attorney General John Ashcroft (a member of the Pentecostal church, the Assemblies of God) attempted to overturn the Oregon Act,[32] arguing that physician-assisted suicide is not a 'legitimate medical purpose' – so begging the question at issue. He ruled that doctors who prescribe drugs to hasten death risked having their medical licences revoked under the Controlled Substances Act 1970. Progressive civil libertarians and conservative states righters united in opposition to the federal intervention, arguing that regulating medical practice was a state matter. Oregon District Court judge Richard Jones blocked the Ashcroft manoeuvre, arguing for the right of states to make their own decisions on matters of medical ethics, and pointing out that the attempt was a perversion of a federal law created to deal with drug abuse and trafficking.

The stated legal basis was the 2001 Supreme Court decision in US v. Oakland Cannabis Buyers' Co-operative,[33] which held that a state could not create its own medical use exception to the CSA's regulation of marihuana. However, marihuana is a

Schedule 1 substance, not subject to the 'legitimate medical purpose' exception applicable to Schedule 2 drugs, such as those
used to hasten death under the Oregon Death with Dignity Act.
Ashcroft ignored this distinction, and overrode the decision of
his predecessor, Attorney General Janet Reno, four years earlier,
who concluded that 'the scope of "legitimate medical use" remained a determination for the state to make, notwithstanding
the unique position of Oregon in end-of-life care.'

The impact of the Ashcroft directive would have been, in violation of the Tenth Amendment, to usurp the traditional state
function of defining 'legitimate medical practice'. It would also
have put the Drug Enforcement Agency in the position of determining whether a specific medical practice was physician-assisted
suicide or terminal sedation, and the likely outcome would have
been additional oversight and scrutiny, and increased use of terminal sedation (as seemingly less problematic).

It is no wonder that the attempt was called 'stunning' (Rogers),
or that it was seen as partisan political adventurism:

> The change in control of the White House in 2001 paved the way for
> a backdoor administrative solution to the perceived problem. The
> mere existence of the OWDA law, one state's bold experiment in
> expanding alternatives available to the terminally ill, was anathema
> to the new executive branch, headed by an avowed opponent of
> end-of-life choice.[34]

This argument has considerable persuasive force, particularly
given recent related federal attempts to encroach into areas of
reproductive rights, but nevertheless it seems to me too simplis-
tic to attribute the action solely to Republican/Democrat partisan
politicisation. Rather, the interesting and important underlying
argument goes to the role of the state.

The state and the individual revisited

The alliance between progressive civil libertarians and conservative state righters may have crossed party lines, but is not as
incongruous as may be supposed. Both groups can trace their
roots to Mill, for the restriction on the role of the state was the
other side of the coin of affirmation of the priority of the individual (discussed in chapter 1). His arguments bear on the ongoing

challenge of balancing change and stability to achieve progress in a society, and concern with the role of government. In *Political Economy*, Mill was quite unequivocal:

> Each is the best judge and guardian of his interests.[35]

'Coleridge' evinced the same concern:

> Beyond suppressing force and fraud, governments can seldom, without doing more harm than good, attempt to chain up the free agency of individuals.[36]

In *On Liberty* Mill gives three reasons for unacceptable state intervention: where the action is better done by individuals; where it is desirable it be done by them as a means of education; and where intervention adds unnecessarily to government power.

Book 5 of *Political Economy* defends a conception of small, unobtrusive government in similar terms as in *On Liberty*:

> There is a circle around every human being, which no government, be it that of one, of a few, or of the many, ought to be permitted to overstep. ... Laissez faire, in short, should be the general practice: every departure from it, unless required by some great good, is a certain evil. ...
>
> It would still remain true that in all the more advanced communities the great majority of things are worse done by the intervention of government, than the individuals most interested in the matter would do them, or cause them to be done if left to themselves.[37]

These arguments apply, and have been influential, much more broadly than in the context of the American constitution.

The recent (2003–4) intervention of Jeb Bush, Governor of Florida, in the Schiavo case[38] suggests that they may need to be reasserted not just at the macro federal level, against the federal government interfering with a state's rights, but also at the micro level of individual states, seeking to intrude into the domain of the individual in a way that is unacceptable to classical Millian liberals.

In America, then, the momentum has moved from refusal of treatment to withdrawal of treatment to letting die to withdrawal of life support to withdrawal of artificial feeding and hydration.

This may seem to exemplify the 'slippery slope' alarmist's worst fears. Has a slippery slope been avoided? This is for the reader to judge. I would argue that it has, for the developments have occurred inexorably over a period of decades, and in a public and contested way, as patient predicaments cried out for resolution. In the Quinlan case, as previously noted, initially the hospital would not grant the patient's request because of the lack of a medical precedent. That ruling settled the issue as far as the withdrawal of life support was concerned, but it took the Cruzan case to extend the scope of the permissible to the removal of artificial nutrition and hydration.

The Oregon Death with Dignity Act set strict eligibility conditions restricted to mentally competent, terminally ill adults, and tight procedural steps, involving two physicians, and counselling, pain management and palliative care as required. No 'right to die' was established in Glucksberg and Quill, and what remains vehemently contested are physician-assisted suicide and euthanasia in the sense of direct killing by medical personnel. Both are opposed by the American Medical Association, and Dworkin[39] and Somerville argue strongly against physician-assisted suicide and deliberate killing as a perversion of the medical role. Yet end-of-life care seems to be a medical matter.

Dworkin endorses allowing to die but opposes deliberate killing, and sees the line blurred in the case of artificial nutrition. Kass caustically deplores the tendency to treat death as a disease, rather than the limiting condition of human life:

> The welcome triumphs against disease have been purchased at the price of the medicalized dehumanization of the end of life: to put it starkly, once we lick cancer and stroke, we can all live long enough to get Alzheimer's disease. And if the insurance holds out, we can die in the intensive care unit, suitably intubated.[40]

He sees three dangers in assisted suicide or euthanasia. Firstly, an obligation on the part of others to kill or help kill. Secondly, in a version of the slippery slope argument, he sees no way to confine the practice to those who knowingly and freely request death. Thirdly, the ethical centre of the medical profession's devotion to heal and refusal to kill will be permanently destroyed, and a personal right will have been bought at the cost of the common good. (As Chairman of the President's Council on Bioethics, his views carry political as well as intellectual weight.)

In response to the first objection, there are no grounds for assuming that patients or doctors will be forced to participate against their will and their conscience any more than in the case of abortion.

Secondly, if the Oregon Death with Dignity Act is taken as the model, as I would recommend, the practice is tightly circumscribed and regulated. If that is where the line is currently drawn, then any cases of physician-assisted suicide outside those guidelines remain a private matter between doctor and patient, which seems appropriate.

Thirdly, the medical mission is to care as well as to cure, and where cure is not possible, caring becomes the primary focus. It may be too much to hope that every patient is known to the doctor, in the old-fashioned 'family doctor' way that is increasingly the exception, but it is surely still incumbent on doctors in any setting to try to ascertain, and then respect, the patient's wishes.

Current medical treatment options of escalating pain relief and sedation are de facto ways to hasten death just as surely as delivering a lethal injection, and can be described as 'letting die' or 'causing to die' as well as 'mercy killing'. The doctor's intention is crucial here, and the figleaf of the double effect doctrine – 'foreseen but unintended consequences' – remains an unsatisfactory smokescreen and in practice leads to undesirable hypocrisy and lack of clarity.

Feminists may find it ironical that this discretion elevates the doctor to the paternalistic position of godlike gatekeeper that was critiqued in the context of medical paternalism in the 1970s.

Feminist ethics developed as a reaction to, and critique of, the Cartesian model of the moral self derived from René Descartes – a disembodied, separate, autonomous, unified self – a rational being essentially similar to all other moral selves, and, implicitly, male. It highlighted the ways Western ethics had excluded women or rationalised their subordination, and criticised the gender blindness and bias in much traditional ethical theory. Though many different approaches flowed from this common starting point, what they held in common was an insistence on the need for contextualisation in ethical theory and social policy, and the need to recognise particularity and difference.

Alison Jaggar, an influential early scholar in the field, articulated three minimal conditions of adequacy for any approach to
ethics that purports to be feminist:

- It must offer a guide to action that will tend to subvert rather
  than reinforce women's subordination.
- It must be able to handle moral issues in both the public and
  private domains.
- It must take the moral experience of all women seriously,
  though not uncritically.

Feminist ethicists pointed out that masculine attributes are val-
ued more highly than feminine ones, and that men have more access to whatever society esteems. Men occupy a position of male
privilege and moral superiority. Carol Gilligan's 1982 challenge[41]
to Lawrence Kohlberg's 1963 hierarchical, analytical and ratio-
nalist model of moral development[42] asserted the 'different voice'
of women and the validity of their concern with feelings and rela-
tionships in making moral judgements. Feminist ethics rejected
the privileging of mind over body characteristic of traditional
ethics, and provided an important paradigm in normative ethics
and epistemology by insisting one cannot simply be human, and
that our social forms are gendered.

In the sphere of bioethics, this approach led to a recognition
of the importance of seeing the broad implications of developments, rather than seeing them as single issues. Who are the
primary caregivers in society? Why is nursing (and social work)
such a female-dominated profession? What power imbalances
are at work here?

Feminist bioethics too did not represent a single approach. A
feminist case was put for in vitro fertilisation (IVF) and surrogacy
in terms of assisting women's liberty, and a feminist case was put
against IVF and surrogacy in terms of the potential to increase
women's oppression. Surrogacy was seen by some to have the
potential to be a new form of class and race colonialism. In both
cases there was seen to be a risk of women losing autonomy in
the face of a paternalistic doctor.

Feminist bioethicists asked the following question: Does reproductive technology enhance a woman's ability to liberate
herself from the expectations and demands placed on women

by society, by exploitation, by restricted role expectations, by marginalisation, and by the normative power of maleness?

Similarly, with medical research as well as reproductive technology, feminist bioethicists consider not only the standard moral questions to do with autonomy, paternalism and justice, but also how the issue in question relates to the oppression of women, and what the implications of a proposed policy would be for the political status of women. They also tend to look at each issue in relation to other practices and assess its structural and systemic implications. Who constructs and maintains an issue? Whose interests are served by it? Is the issue part of a structure that confines or empowers a particular group?

Feminist bioethicists are therefore likely to be extremely cautious about any developments in relation to physician-assisted suicide, euthanasia and end-of-life decision-making that place the doctor in the potentially paternalistic position of gatekeeper, and are likely to be particularly sensitive to safeguards that protect the patient's autonomy in a situation of extreme vulnerability.

When so much that is sought by advocates of physician-assisted suicide and euthanasia is allowed under 'medical treatment', particularly bolstered by the double effect doctrine, very little that is desired remains beyond the pale – clearly, smothering the patient. The distinctions become virtually without substance.

Certainly, the American public do not seem to make much of the distinction between euthanasia and physician-assisted suicide, supporting both at the same rate (65 per cent), though they do distinguish between withdrawing life support and providing pain medications, even with the increased risk of respiratory depression and death: 90 per cent deem that ethical.

There appears to be a consensus that emphasis on care and human dignity are paramount, and that end-of-life medical care must remain anchored in and governed by the express wishes of the patient – expressed either at the time or in an advance directive. This is where cleavage points arise, as concern is expressed about the importance of not abandoning those who do not fit the profile of mentally competent, terminally ill adults. Amarasekama[43] even goes so far as to argue that it is discriminatory to so limit access to physician-assisted suicide and euthanasia. This is not a 'slippery slope' fear of extension of the currently acceptable, but a demand that it be extended. This boundary problem was addressed in the Philosophers' Brief.

The only answer for now may be that mentally competent, terminally ill adults must remain the target group, as consensus here is all that can currently be secured.

Dworkin has provided powerful arguments as to why this group remains the priority. He argues that we die in the shadow of our whole lives, and 'none of us wishes to end our lives out of character'. It is, he asserts, a 'devastating, odious form of tyranny' to make someone die 'in a way that others approve, but he believes a horrifying contradiction of his life' – or, by extension, would so believe if he was conscious of it. He also dismisses as invalid the assumption that no serious harm is done keeping alive someone who wants to die.

As Dworkin unforgettably puts it, we also dread life as 'an unthinking yet scrupulously tended vegetable'. He puts the challenge in classical liberal terms:

> The community must decide how far to permit its members to choose death.

However, he raises the related question of whether any political community should make intrinsic values a matter of collective decision rather than individual choice:

> The critical question is whether a decent society will choose coercion or responsibility, whether it will seek to impose a collective judgement on matters of the most profound spiritual character on everyone, or whether it will allow and ask its citizens to make the most central, personality-defining judgements about their own lives themselves.[44]

What role, then, should the state play? Should it opt out entirely and leave regulation of end-of-life issues to the medical profession? Surely not. The courts have a valuable role to play in articulating the issues involved in problematic, cutting-edge cases – cases that will continue to arise in the wake of medical and scientific advances. National regulation is important and desirable, so that patients are not forced to play off one state against another, or become 'death tourists',[45] or go through a long and expensive hierarchy of legal appeals. The rule of law is vital to a democratic society. The law should represent community consensus, be 'owned' by the community and change in

response to changing community attitudes. It would also clar-
ify the situation, and what is permissible for both doctors and
nurses – frequently the ones closest to the patients, but without
the authority to prescribe or alter pain relief.[46]

Opinions differ. Dworkin argues that for reasons of beneficence as well as autonomy, the state should not impose uni-
form general laws. Somerville favours leaving legislation against
physician-assisted suicide and euthanasia on the statute books,
but not prosecuting. Others favour having an approved defence
such as 'compassionate and caring medical practice' or 'mercy
killing'; this has been a successful defence for family members as
well as medical practitioners.

In my view, a mixed regime is best, one that balances legislation like the Oregon Death with Dignity Act, which sets out
ground rules and specifies acceptable conditions, with oversight
farmed out to the medical profession. This would suggest that a
finding of professional misconduct was the first resort and probably sufficient in the majority of cases, particularly as the American and Australian Medical Associations remain opposed. This
would still leave the option of pressing criminal charges.

Legislation could be both clarifying and empowering. Janet
Adkins was an Oregon woman suffering early Alzheimer's in
1989. Knowing what lay ahead of her, she met Dr Kevorkian in
Michigan with her husband and two sons. After a night thinking
things over and with family support, she met Dr Kevorkian again
and confirmed her wish to 'get out with dignity'. Two days later,
she entered the back of his Volkswagon van. Unable to find her
a room, he had installed a bed and a suicide machine there – the
suicide machine allowed patients to kill themselves by pressing
a button that injects poison through a needle the doctor has
earlier inserted in a vein. Janet Adkins pressed the button and
died.

Dr Kevorkian was prosecuted for murder, but the charge was
dismissed because he had not done anything other than help
Janet Adkins commit suicide, and that was not against the law.
In 1992 Michigan made such machines illegal; the law came into
effect in March 1993. Adkins is an example of a conscious and
competent patient who at fifty-four could still beat her thirty-
year-old son at tennis, but could no longer keep score. She made
a competent decision to die, to forestall becoming incompetent.
Had she had the power to direct in advance that she be killed at

a certain point, she may have had years of additional life before reaching the stage she dreaded.

This is true of all progressive diseases and would seem to be a strong argument for people to direct in advance what they consider the boundary while they still can, before they become incompetent. This is not entirely unproblematic, however, as shown by the case of *Knight* v. *Beverley Health Care Center*,[47] where James Cameron, the husband of Delores Cameron (who had suffered a stroke), requested that her feeding tube be removed as her living will directed once she was diagnosed as in a 'permanent vegetative state'. Her sons, Vernon and William Knight, objected to the feeding tube being removed.

Advance directives, however deal only with withdrawal of treatment and normally cover matters such as coronary-pulmonary resuscitation and intravenous feeding, surgical or intensive care, in the context of what irreversible condition the patient considers intolerable, so that he would want only palliative care. The right to request 'aid in dying' at a time and place of the patient's choice, after two physicians have certified that death will occur within six months, has been proposed in draft statutes, which California rejected in 1992 and Washington state in 1991. It is possible that the law will in future move in this direction, but a major paradigm shift is needed. Perhaps the most likely outcome is that with the increased normalisation of use and acceptance of advance directives, their scope will be extended to encompass 'aid in dying'.

The preceding discussion of Janet Adkins has dealt with a patient who would be deemed 'conscious and competent' in Dworkin's three-way classification.[48] Previous discussion centred on the 'unconscious and incompetent' patients Karen Quinlan and Nancy Cruzan. It is the third category, 'conscious but incompetent', that remains problematic. It is the prospect of involuntary euthanasia being extended to these patients that 'slippery slope' alarmists invoke. What guidance is available to reassure euthanasia sceptics that banning euthanasia is not the only safeguard?

Earlier, the position of Mill and his commitment to liberty and choice were described, and it is his position, I believe, that provides the best way forward in this contentious area. The perspective taken in this book is therefore a Millian utilitarian standpoint. Mill asserts that utility, or the greatest happiness principle,

is the foundation of morals, and that actions are right as they tend
to promote happiness, and wrong as they tend to produce the reverse of happiness. Mill argues for 'utility in the largest sense,
grounded in the permanent interests of man as a progressive
being',[49] and from this derived the distinction between higher
and lower pleasures that led him to stress individuality, choice
and self-determination as central to human nature, and to argue for the largest possible sphere of liberty and autonomy for
such a person – a rational, competent adult. It is such a person
who exemplifies human dignity and is worthy of respect. The
conscious, competent patient may be seen as the paradigm of
this fuller notion of the human person, while the poor quality of
life available to the unconscious and incompetent individual in a
persistent vegetative state (who can no longer be considered an
individual on this account) is a justification, as we have seen, for
not continuing to keep such a patient alive.

Yet there are some implications for the conscious and incompetent patient as well. The Alzheimer's disease sufferer should be
seen not as a demented person, but as a person who has become
demented, and must be considered in the light of the whole of
their life and their past competent self. Even if they are no longer
a person in the fully fledged sense, as a human being they still
should be treated in a way that accords them dignity, and have
a right not to suffer indignity.

Mill points out that his account of human nature is meant to
apply only to 'human beings in the maturity of their faculties ...
not children or young persons below the age which the law may
fix as that of manhood or womanhood'.[50]

But still, the account is strong enough and the synergy between a progressive society and progressive individuals powerful enough to persuade us to treat people as far as possible as if
they exemplified this ideal, even if they no longer do, or, in other
cases, such as severely disabled newborns or others, never have.
It is for our sake as a society, as well as theirs. The number of
Alzheimer's patients is expected to increase with the ageing of
society, so it is not only the common good, but our own possible
future that urges us to careful and compassionate consideration
of what we as a society endorse in this area. This is what is en-
tailed by respect for persons, for human dignity, which is a core
value of a liberal democratic society and can best be affirmed in
legislation.

Moreover, the medical principle of beneficence entails that the doctor act in the patient's best interests. This is akin to a fiduciary duty, and can be monitored in the same way as other fiduciary duties.

It is not necessary, I would maintain, to ban euthanasia on the basis of slippery slope fears for the vulnerable, the demented or the incompetent, but rather carefully and conscientiously to use the full regulatory apparatus of legislation, medical case committees, hospital ethics committees, consultations with family, carers and guardians, and, if necessary, the public guardian, in making end-of-life decisions for this problematic group of conscious but incompetent patients.

The guidelines indicated are intuitive and situational, but they do constitute robust guidelines to apply and to help draw defensible lines to frame and resolve the cases which are particularly problematic in this always difficult area.

It is likely that America will continue to produce new cutting-edge cases. This chapter has traced the evolution of the debate in America over room for choice over death since the 1968 Harvard brain death criterion revolutionised understanding of what constituted death, as well as medical practice in dealing with it.

The American Constitution has been cited as grounding a tendency to argue in terms of rights. Arguments in terms of liberty and autonomy have been preferred, and have been examined in relation to three groups of people: the conscious and competent; the unconscious and incompetent; and (most problematic of all) the conscious and incompetent.

As far as the role of the state in regulating this contentious area is concerned, of all the regulatory options available, it would seem that the normalisation of advance directives may be the only likely means of breaching the current opposition to physician-assisted suicide and euthanasia.

Notes

1. M. J. Silviera et al., 'Patients' Knowledge of Options at the End of Life', *JAMA* Vol. 284, No. 19 (2000).
2. J. Rawls et al., 'Assisted Suicide: The Philosophers' Brief', *The New York Review of Books* (27 March 1997).
3. N. M. Gorsuch, 'The Right to Assisted Suicide and Euthanasia', *Harvard Journal of Law and Public Policy* Vol. 23, No. 3 (2000): 607.
4. Ibid.

5. Ibid., p. 610.
6. Ibid., p. 611.
7. R. T. Hull, 'The Case for Physician-Assisted Suicide', *Free Inquiry* Vol. 23, No. 3 (2003).
8. Rawls et al., 'Assisted Suicide: The Philosophers' Brief', p. 47.
9. Ibid.
10. Ibid., p. 433.
11. A. Maslow, *Toward a Psychology of Being* (New York: Van Nostrand, 1968); idem, *The Farther Reaches of Human Nature* (Harmondsworth: Penguin, 1971).
12. M. Nussbaum, *Women and Human Development* (Cambridge: Cambridge University Press, 2000).
13. M. Nussbaum and J. Glover, *Women, Culture and Development* (Oxford: Clarendon Press, 1995).
14. L. R. Kass, *Life, Liberty and the Defense of Dignity* (San Francisco: Encounter Books, 2002), p. 213.
15. Ibid., p. 214.
16. Ibid.
17. Ibid., p. 215.
18. T. Sheldon, 'Dutch GP Cleared after Helping to End Man's "Hopeless Existence"', *British Medical Journal* Vol. 321, No. 11 (November 2000); T. Sheldon, 'Being "Tired of Life" is not Grounds for Euthanasia', *British Medical Journal* Vol. 326 (2003).
19. Gorsuch, 'The Right to Assisted Suicide and Euthanasia'; S. Horsfall et al., 'Views of Euthanasia from an East Texas University', *Social Science Journal* Vol. 38 (2001).
20. R. McStay, 'Terminal Sedation: Palliative Care for Intractable Pain, Post-Glucksberg and Quill', *American Journal of Law and Medicine* Vol. 29, No. 1 (2003).
21. Somerville, *Death Talk*.
22. B. R. Sharma, 'To Legalize Physician-Assisted Suicide or Not? – a Dilemma', *Journal of Clinical Forensic Medicine* Vol. 10 (2003).
23. M. Cosic, *The Right to Die?* (Melbourne: New Holland Publishers, 2003), p. 137.
24. Horsfall et al., 'Views of Euthanasia from an East Texas University'.
25. T. Quill, 'Death and Dignity: A Case of Individualised Decision', *New England Journal of Medicine* Vol. 324 (1991).
26. Cosic, *The Right to Die?*, p. 142.
27. H. R. Glick and A. Hutchinson, 'The Rising Agenda of Physician-Assisted Suicide', *Policy Studies Journal* Vol. 27 (2004).
28. P. Paul, 'Euthanasia and Assisted Suicide', *American Demographics* (November 2002).
29. R. Watson, 'First Belgian to Use New Euthanasia Law Provokes Storm of Protest', *Belgian Medical Journal* Vol. 325 (2002).
30. Quill, 'Death and Dignity: A Case of Individualised Decision'.
31. L. A. Roscoe et al., 'A Comparison of Characteristics of Kevorkian

Euthanasia Cases and Physician-Assisted Suicides in Oregon', *The Gerontologist* Vol. 41, No. 4 (2001).

32. N. Lund, 'Why Ashcroft is Wrong on Assisted Suicide', *Commentary* Vol. 113, No. 2 (2002); Adam Liptak, 'Ruling Upholds Oregon Law Authorising Assisted Suicide', *New York Times* (27 May 2004).

33. E. H. Rogers, 'A Federalism of Convenience', *Human Rights* Vol. 29, No. 4 (Fall 2002).

34. Ibid., p. 15.

35. J. S. Mill, *Collected Works*, Vol. 11, p. 404.

36. Ibid., Vol. X, p. 156.

37. Ibid., p. 941.

38. Abby Goodnough, 'Governor of Florida Orders Woman Fed in Right-to-Die Case', *New York Times* (22 October 2003).

39. R. Dworkin, *Life's Dominion* (London: HarperCollins, 1998); Somerville, *Death Talk*.

40. Kass, *Life, Liberty and the Defense of Dignity*, p. 226.

41. C. Gilligan, *In a Different Voice* (Cambridge, MA: Harvard University Press, 1982).

42. L. Kohlberg, *The Philosophy of Moral Development: Moral Stages and the Idea of Justice* (San Francisco: Harper & Row, 1981).

43. Kumar Amarasekara, 'Autonomy, Paternalism and Discrimination: The Darker Side of Euthanasia', in *Legal Visions of the 21st Century*, ed. A. Angie and G. Sturgess (The Hague: Kluwer Law International, 1998).

44. Dworkin, *Life's Dominion*, p. 216.

45. A. Langley, ' "Suicide Tourists" Go to the Swiss for Help in Dying', *New York Times* 2003; G. Naik, 'Last Requests: The Grim Mission of a Swiss Group: Visitors' Suicides', *Wall Street Journal* (22 November 2002).

46. D. A. Asch et al., 'The Limits of Suffering: Critical Care Nurses' Views of Hospital Care at the End of Life', *Social Science Medicine* Vol. 45, No. 11 (1997).

47. Barry A. Bostrom, '*Knight* v. *Beverly Health Care Centre*: In the Supreme Court of Alabama', *Issues in Law and Medicine* Vol. 17, No. 2 (2001).

48. Dworkin, *Life's Dominion*, pp. 183, 189 and 192.

49. G. Tulloch, *Mill and Sexual Equality* (Brighton: Harvester-Wheatsheaf, 1989), p. 148.

50. Mill, *Collected Works*, Vol. XVIII, p. 224.

4

Legal Disputes over Death in England

We have seen in chapter 3 how issues of choice and death are contested in America, a country with a constitution, a federal government and fifty state governments. England presents a very different and more unified landscape, while also providing some of the early key cases, dating back to the 1950s.

The Devlin doctrine

In 1957 Dr John Bodkin Adams gave an injection that shortened the life of his elderly patient, Mrs Morrell. A sensational trial ensued in which it was alleged that Dr Adams had persuaded Mrs Morrell to leave him money and valuables in her will. Dr Adams countered that he was merely easing her agony. Justice (later Lord) Devlin directed the jury that 'a doctor is entitled to do all that is proper and necessary to relieve pain and suffering, even if the measures he takes may incidentally shorten life'.[1] This reflects the 'foreseen but unintended effect' doctrine (discussed in chapter 3), on the basis that to foresee that an act may shorten someone's life is not the same as to intend to shorten that person's life. Given that the outcome is the same this may seem casuistical, but it is an important view and remains the policy of the American and Australian Medical Associations today, nearly fifty years later. This itself may seem surprising in the light of Lord Devlin's famed social conservatism, medical developments and the passage of time.

In passing, Justice Devlin had noted the condition 'if the purpose of medicine, the restoration to health, can no longer be achieved', there is still much for a doctor to do, and he is entitled to do all that is proper and necessary to relieve pain and suffering, even if the measures he takes may incidentally shorten life.

> This is not because there is a special defence for medical men but because no act is murder which does not cause death. We are not dealing here with the philosophical or technical cause, but with the commonsense cause. The cause of death is the illness or the injury, and the proper medical treatment that is administered and that has an incidental effect on determining the exact moment of death is not the cause of death in any sensible use of the term.[2]

Devlin concluded unequivocally against deliberate killing:

> It remains the fact, and it remains the law, that no doctor, nor any man, no more in the case of the dying than of the healthy, has the right deliberately to cut the thread of life.[3]

In Justice Devlin's view, then, it is the intention to end life that marks the boundary between murder and sound medical practice. (This is reflected in definitions of murder in statutes such as the Crimes Act in New South Wales, which includes not only acts, but also omissions, if done with the intent to end life.) What is affirmed is that it is always wrong intentionally to end an innocent human life.

Adams' act may be seen as reprehensible across all the distinctions cited in chapter 3: it was an act, not an omission; it involved killing, not letting die; it involved extraordinary, not ordinary means; and it was a case of intending, not merely foreseeing death. Devlin thus gave a clear statement of the traditional view, which was momentously modified in the Bland case of 1989. Before looking at that, we should examine the case of Dr Nigel Cox, which occurred over thirty years after Dr Adams. In 1992, Dr Cox a hospital doctor, not a GP, was tried for injecting a double dose of potassium chloride (which has no curative or painkilling properties) in addition to a dose of heroin into his patient, Mrs Boyes, who had suffered from rheumatoid arthritis for twenty years and, in excruciating pain, was close to death. Her two sons were with her and supported her request. Dr Cox was reported to the police after a Roman Catholic nurse read the notes and reported him to hospital management. Mrs Boyes' body had been cremated, so there was no direct evidence of cause of death. Dr Cox was charged with attempted murder and found guilty. Nevertheless, he was given a twelve-month suspended sentence and was not struck off the medical register. This would seem to indicate strong official and unofficial sympathy for such a demonstrable case of 'mercy killing' (he had no financial incentive), and an undermining of the monolithic façade of the traditional view. This was further challenged by the Bland case.

The Tony Bland case

The circumstances of the Tony Bland case were tragic. In 1989, the seventeen-year-old football fan went to Hillsborough Football Stadium for an FA Cup semi-final. Supporters were crowding into the ground as the match started and a fatal crush ensued, when fans were pushed against the security fencing. Ninety-five people died. Tony Bland's lungs were crushed and his brain was deprived of oxygen; only his brain stem survived. He fell into a persistent vegetative state: such patients may survive from ten to thirty years. For three and a half years his body was maintained by artificial hydration and nutrition via a nasogastric tube.

His condition, as described by Lord Justice Hoffman, was heartrending:

> Since April 15 1989 Anthony Bland has been in persistent vegetative state. He lies in Airedale General Hospital in Keighley, fed liquid food by a pump through a tube passing through his nose and down the back of his throat into his stomach. His bladder is emptied through a catheter inserted through his penis, which from time to time has caused infections requiring dressing and antibiotic treatment. His stiffened joints have caused his limbs to be rigidly contracted so that his arms are tightly flexed across his chest and his legs unnaturally contorted. Reflex movements in the throat cause him to vomit and dribble. Of all this, and the presence of members of his family who take turns to visit him, Anthony Bland has no consciousness at all. *The parts of his brain which provide him with consciousness have turned to fluid.* The darkness and oblivion which descended at Hillsborough will never depart. His body is alive, but he has no life in the sense that even the most pitifully handicapped but conscious human being has a life. But the advances of modern medicine permit him to be kept in this state for years, even perhaps for decades. (my emphasis)[4]

In that last sentence lies the nub of the problem.

Neither his family nor his doctors could see any benefit in keeping him alive in such a state, and in November 1992 the Airedale Hospital Trust petitioned the High Court for permission to withdraw hydration and nutrition. The case was appealed in December 1992, and, on 4 February 1993, to the House of Lords. Significantly, as Britain has neither a written constitution nor a federal system of government (unlike the United States) the House of Lords could not avoid dealing with the case. Their decision was momentous. Where all three courts had found it unlawful to discontinue feeding, the House of Lords ruled that artificial hydration and nutrition constituted medical treatment and that a doctor had no duty to continue treatment where it would be of no benefit, and particularly when it was invasive and had not been consented to. On 22 February, antibiotics and feeding were discontinued, and Tony Bland died nine days later.

While other cases had endorsed the discontinuation of treatment which was not beneficial, and thus allowed patients to die, what was significant in the Tony Bland case was that he was not dying in the accepted sense, and that food and drink were deemed to constitute medical treatment and not normal care.[5]

This action contrasts with the lack of action of the US Supreme Court in the similar case of Nancy Cruzan, where life-sustaining treatment could initially not be terminated because Cruzan was not competent to refuse treatment herself.

Critics held that the House of Lords had legalised euthanasia. Singer, on the contrary, hails it as a breach in the sanctity of life doctrine in that here British law formally abandoned the idea that life itself is a benefit, irrespective of its quality. Singer drew the conclusion that in this case, the law held that for life to be of benefit to the person living it, that person must, as a minimum, have some capacity for awareness or consciousness. Furthermore, it was obvious that the proposal to discontinue the tube feeding and hydration was intended to bring about Tony Bland's death – a viewpoint markedly at loggerheads with Devlin's judgment in Adams (see p. 81 and chapter 3).

In fact nine judges (one in the Family Division of the High Court, three in the Court of Appeal, and five in the House of Lords) each made it clear that he did not value human life that is only life in a biological sense.

Lord Justice Butler-Sloss of the Court of Appeal explicitly balanced sanctity of life against quality of life:

> The considerations as to the quality of life of Mr Bland now and in the future in his extreme situation are in my opinion rightly to be placed on the other side of the crucial equation from the general principle of the sanctity and inviolability of life. In this appeal those factors which include the reality of Mr Bland's existence outweigh the abstract requirement to preserve life.[6]

Lord Justice Hoffman attempted to rebut the implication he was making a quality of life decision, when the Official Solicitor claimed a decision allowing Bland to die would be a decision that his life was not worth living:

> There is no question of his life being worth living or not worth living, because the stark reality is that Anthony Bland is not living a life at all.[7]

Legally, however, Bland was alive, and a decision to let him die made sense only on the view that mere biological existence was not worth living.

The Lords took the same view. Lord Keith of Kinkel referred to 'a permanently insensate being' and concluded:

> It is, however, perhaps permissible to say that to an individual with no cognitive capacity whatever, and no prospect of ever recovering any such capacity in this world, it must be a matter of complete indifference whether he lives or dies.[8]

Lord Goff of Chieveley described as futile medical treatment 'simply to prolong a patient's life' if the patient is unconscious and there is no prospect of improvement in his condition. Lord Lowrey agreed, concluding, 'it is not in the interest of an insensate patient to continue life-supporting care and treatment'.

Lord Mustil concluded that withdrawal of life support was not only legally but ethically justified, 'since the continued treatment of Anthony Bland can no longer serve to maintain that combination of manifold characteristics which we call a personality'.

Lord Browne-Wilkinson thought the decision whether continued treatment was beneficial was for doctors to make; the court had only to decide whether the responsible doctors had reached a reasonable belief. In this case he found it 'perfectly reasonable' for the doctors to conclude that maintaining Bland's life brought him 'no affirmative benefit'. Importantly, he also expressed concern about the legal framework:

> How could it be lawful to allow a patient to die slowly, though painlessly, over a period of weeks from lack of food, but unlawful to produce his immediate death by lethal injection, thereby saving his family from yet another ordeal? [It is] ... difficult to find a moral answer to that question. But it is undoubtedly the law that the doing of a positive act with the intention of ending a life is ... and remains murder.[9]

Killing and letting die revisited

The last sentence restated the Devlin view. What Lord Browne-Wilkinson was alluding to was the 1992 conviction of Dr Nigel Cox, when Dr Cox received a suspended twelve-month jail term for the attempted murder of Mrs Boyes. As Campbell points out, Lord Browne-Wilkinson had raised a very central and challenging question:

> Why is it permissible to cease to provide a patient in a permanent vegetative state with what he needs to stay alive, but not permissible to provide a patient with what she needs to die – particularly given the permanent vegetative state patient did not consent to the withdrawal of the life-preserving care, and the other patient had repeatedly begged her doctor for the injection he finally administered?[10]

The distinction, apparently, was that Tony Bland was not to be killed, but allowed to die, whereas Dr Cox had killed Mrs Boyes.

The Law Lords in Bland authorised the non-treatment of the patient, knowing it would lead to his death, on the following arguments:

- A doctor is under no duty to continue to treat a patient where such treatment confers no benefit on the patient.
- Being in a persistent vegetative state with no prospect of recovery is not regarded by informed medical opinion as being a benefit to a patient.

- The principle of the sanctity of life was not absolute, for example:
    a) where a patient expressly refuses treatment, even though death may well be a consequence of that refusal;
    b) where a prisoner on hunger strike refuses food and may not be forcibly fed;
    c) where a patient is terminally ill, death is imminent and treatment will only prolong suffering.

Artificial hydration and nutrition required medical intervention for its application and was widely regarded by the medical profession as medical treatment.

The relevant principle was not that it was permissible to let a patient die, provided he was not actually killed; rather it was that caring for a patient did not require futile medical intervention – that is, of no benefit to the patient.

Lord Justice Butler-Sloss also drew a contrast between Cox and Bland:

> The position of Dr Nigel Cox, who injected a lethal dose designed to cause death, was different since it was an external and intrusive act and was not in accord with his duty of care as a doctor. The distinction between Mr Bland's doctors and Dr Cox was between an act or omission which allowed causes already present in the body to operate and the introduction of an external agency of death.[11]

This statement begged the very question at issue – whether Dr Cox's action was in accord with his duty of care as a doctor. *The Guardian* at the time dismissed this view as 'philosophical nonsense'. One might take this view on the grounds that the law of homicide provides that omissions as well as acts fall within its scope. There also seems no moral reason for holding one less culpable for the adverse effects of not doing something one ought to have done than for the ill effects of doing something one ought not to have done. As we have seen, the outcome may be the same and the intent may be the same.

Robert Campbell seeks an explanation in the need to draw a line of principle. As he points out, since the early 1970s the UK prison service has held to a policy of not force-feeding hunger strikers, even if their lives are in danger. Some prisoners – famously, the IRA prisoner Bobby Sands in Northern Ireland – have died as a result. This policy acknowledges the Millian principle that over this area of their life individual sovereignty is sacrosanct and society has no business to intervene. Yet it is not permissible to assist them, for this would be to move into the area of euthanasia, which remains illegal in the UK and most other legal jurisdictions.

Campbell argues that this is not a defensible position, as it is not normally the case that it is an offence to assist someone to do something it would not be wrong for them to do themselves.

This is indeed the nub of whether there is a defensible line to be drawn between voluntary euthanasia and physician-assisted suicide other than a firmly held view that this is a professional breach of the doctor's role. Lack of a rational, defensible distinction between suicide and euthanasia creates pressure for legalisation of voluntary euthanasia. There would then be no need to try to draw a distinction between Bland and Cox cases.

Campbell concedes legal and moral prohibitions on killing must cut in somewhere, and so a line must be drawn. Adopting Bernard Williams' distinction between reasonable and effective distinctions, Campbell argues a distinction may be justifiable on rational grounds, but impossible to enforce; or it may not stand philosophical scrutiny, but be accepted and understood. In a classic 'baldness and hairiness' argument, he points out that it is hard to defend any material difference between someone of seventeen years and eleven months and an eighteen-year-old. But a clear point at which maturity is attained is a practical necessity in any society – even if different societies draw the line at different ages. So he accepts there may be good policy reasons for distinguishing between suicide and euthanasia or between withdrawing treatment and killing, as popular morality currently does, even if moral grounds are harder to find or justify. Given the hope that policy may be based on sound moral grounds, this is a grudging concession to the status quo, rather than a distinction based on principle.

Campbell stresses the importance of patient consent in matters of treatment, and not only because treating a patient without consent is a battery. Even more importantly, treatment is only partly a medical matter. In Millian terms, Campbell points out that the patient is 'the only specialist on her own life'. However, there is a gap between a competent patient's right to refuse treatment and a right to voluntary euthanasia. A right to decline treatment that may keep you alive does not imply a right to demand treatment that will kill you or to force another to assist. Legally, you are not wronged by something you have consented to, barring criminal injuries.

As for the competent patient's right to refuse treatment, the case of Frances Pollack in 2002 suggests that it too is not unproblematic. Frances Pollack, an English former nurse, was featured in the media when she had 'DNR' (Do Not Resuscitate) tattooed on her chest to ensure she was not resuscitated against her will in an emergency, despite carrying a directive to that effect in her wallet.

The most important question the Bland case raises is that of whether caring for patients always requires that we continue to treat them. Both the Anglican church and the Roman Catholic church have acknowledged there is no duty to treat when cure is impossible.

If care is taken as the paramount priority in medicine, as I have argued it should be, then Dr Cox was in a bind where cure was impossible and discontinuing the pain relief only exacerbated the situation and would not have led to Mrs Boyes' death – as did the discontinuation of treatment for Tony Bland.

Campbell finds it hard to support the argument that that Cox did anything wrong, and suggests that he was prosecuted because a line had to be drawn somewhere – and while this may be legally enforceable and practically effective, it is not morally defensible. Moreover, such a course only encourages ad hoc adjustments such as acquittal or a suspended sentence.

Euthanasia in 1994 and 2004

In 1994 the House of Lords issued a three-volume report on euthanasia. The report recognised the importance of the autonomy of the individual and the universal desire to relieve extreme suffering, but concluded the arguments in favour of voluntary euthanasia were not sufficient to weaken society's commitment to the sanctity of life and the prohibition on intentional killing of the innocent. In Devlinesque terms, it affirmed that prohibition is 'the cornerstone of law and social relations'.

We believe that the issue of euthanasia is one in which the interest of the individual cannot be separated from the interest of society as a whole. ... To create an exception to the general prohibition of in-tentional killing would inevitably open the way to its further erosion whether by design, by inadvertence, or by the human tendency to test the limits of any regulation.[12]

This was essentially a slippery slope argument, and while the re-port upheld the individual's long-recognised right to refuse treat-ment, the matter of voluntary euthanasia was effectively closed in the United Kingdom.

The Diane Pretty case

Pressure to reconsider the issue came from the Diane Pretty case.[13] In 2000 Diane Pretty was diagnosed with motor neurone disease, an incurable progressive disease of the nervous system. In August 2001 she petitioned the Director of Public Prosecutions for an assurance that her husband would not be charged if he helped her to commit suicide (the Suicide Act 1961 decriminalised suicide, but made it a crime, punishable by up to fourteen years in prison, for anyone to assist).[14] Though the Director expressed his sympathy, he upheld the law. The Prettys' legal team argued that this discriminated against the disabled and took their case to the High Court, which upheld the Director of Public Prosecution's decision, as did the House of Lords. The House of Lords held that neither the courts nor the Director of Public Prosecutions had the power to suspend or dispense with laws in the UK, and though it is not an offence to attempt suicide, it is to assist it[15] (as in Australia and the Nancy Crick case: see chapter 7).

In a precedent-setting move, the Prettys then appealed to the European Court of Human Rights, as the European Convention on Human Rights had been subsumed into UK law under the Human Rights Act 1988. The Prettys appeared in Strasbourg in March 2002, arguing that the British law infringed five articles of the European Convention on Human Rights – specifically, those that demand respect for private life, and prohibit inhumane or degrading treatment. The seven European judges again expressed sympathy, but dismissed the claim. They also affirmed:

Cogent reasons exist for not seeking to distinguish between those able and unable to commit suicide unaided. The borderline between the two categories would often be a very fine one, and to seek to build into the law (such an exemption) would seriously undermine the protection of life which the 1961 Act was intended to safeguard, and greatly increase the risk of abuse.[16]

The Court recognised that Diane Pretty was not the type of vulnerable person the prohibition on assisted suicide is intended to protect, but found that flexibility in a particular situation was sufficiently catered for by the discretion of the Director of Public Prosecution whether to prosecute and the power of the municipal court to impose a lesser sentence.

The EU practice of allowing member states a 'margin of appreciation'[17] in determining rights claims by reference to the norms of a particular society meant that the English prohibition on assisted suicide was allowed to stand. A claim from a different jurisdiction might have been resolved differently; or in cases with a wide divergence of national practices, the Court will allow a substantially greater margin of appreciation. So future rulings of the Court in this area will be determined by developments across Europe in relation to the domestic regulation of euthanasia – whether it be restrictive or permissive.[18]

Ironically, the day Diane Pretty lost her case in Strasbourg, another woman, Miss B, died peacefully in hospital after winning a case to have her life support removed.[19] In an echo of Bland and Cox, Miss B's exercise of her right to refuse treatment amounted to a decision to die. Like Mrs Boyes, the only treatment available to Diane Pretty was pain relief and there was no treatment she could suspend to hasten death.

Diane Pretty's case attracted considerable media coverage and aroused tremendous sympathy before her death in May 2002 by suffocation – as she had feared – two weeks after the Strasbourg ruling. Her widower presented the British Prime Minister with a petition signed by 50,000 people calling for the legalisation of voluntary euthanasia and assisted suicide.

Doyal and Doyal, writing in *The British Medical Journal* immediately after the Strasbourg ruling,[20] argued that the decision, while consistent with legal precedent, was morally wrong and that the law should be changed. In the face of so much moral right, they ask, where is the wrong?

Baroness Warnock came to the same conclusion. In a dramatic example of the effect of the case, Baroness Warnock, the moral philosopher and Chair of the Warnock Committee's

1984 Report of the Committee of Inquiry into Human Fertilisation and Embryology (which became a model around the world), wrote a prominent article in *The Sunday Times* in December 2003, entitled 'I made a bad law – we should help the ill to die'.[21]

Warnock took as her starting point the fact that she was a member of the House of Lords committee which ten years earlier had rejected legalising euthanasia, and in the context that a House of Lords Select Committee was about to be set up to consider the issue of assisted suicide.

The House of Lords committee that Warnock referred to concluded that the law should not be changed, and that assisted death should remain a civil offence unless a decision were made in court making it permissible for a patient to die in very particular circumstances, such as for a permanent vegetative state patient whose life-support machine is to be turned off. Warnock says that 'a great deal was made at the time of the distinction between killing and allowing to die' and that 'this seemed to me a wholly bogus distinction'. She went along with the committee's conclusions, conscious that the arguments were suspect and that the conclusions were not written in stone. She believed then that the medical and nursing professions would have to face the fact that being alive was, in certain circumstances, contrary to a patient's wishes and interests, and that palliative care, even if available, could not render the patient's suffering endurable. As previously noted (chapter 2), palliative care virtually originated in the United Kingdom with the work of Dame Cicely Saunders, founder of the hospice movement.

The new euthanasia committee is the outcome of a Private Member's Bill introduced into the House of Lords by Lord Joffe. Its scope is extremely limited. It proposes that those who are terminally ill and in sight of death and suffering severely, but are of sound mind and have expressed a wish to die before their condition becomes even more unbearable, may be assisted to die, without the risk that whoever assists them – doctor, friend or family member – will be charged with murder. The Assisted Dying For The Terminally Ill Bill (HL) is currently at the reading stage.

Warnock cites Diane Pretty's case as one that partly motivated these proposals. She personally was affected by the death of her husband, the moral philosopher Geoffrey Warnock, from a progressive and incurable lung disease, fibrosing alveolitis. Like

Diane Pretty he had a horror of suffocating, which he knew would be the manner of his death. In this case, he was in the care of the family GP, who, Warnock supposes, increased his dose of morphine. Warnock is sure that what he did was right, and that in acting from compassion, he exemplified the deep motive of the medical profession at its best.

Not only is the proposed bill limited in extent. It provides that more than one doctor would have to agree that all the conditions were satisfied.

Warnock notes that some would oppose the Bill on absolute grounds, generally from religious belief, and contends, in a traditional liberal argument, that the law cannot be determined by a particular religious belief:

> There must exist moral considerations behind the law separate from religion (even if influenced by it) deriving their authority from our idea of the common good.

She points out that arguments against the Bill put forward by those of no dogmatic faith usually take the form of the so-called slippery slope argument. Warnock counters that 'the whole point of legislation is to place an immovable barrier to prevent our slipping further down it'. If Joffe's Bill proposed a new category of death called mercy killing, she could see the force of the slippery slope argument and would oppose it, but it does not. Assisted suicide is different. She argues that the medical profession should be trusted to observe the criteria laid down in the Bill. If they do not, they should be prosecuted.

What is envisaged, then, is legislation backed up by oversight by the medical profession.

Warnock acknowledges that there may be difficulties in ensuring the criteria are indeed satisfied, but argues that this difficulty should not be used to prevent relief for clear-cut cases like Diane Pretty's.

These developments might be grounds for optimism, were it not for Dr Harold Shipman,[22] who I fear has caused a tremendous setback to progressive reconsideration of voluntary euthanasia and physician-assisted suicide, and has aroused atavistic fears of murderous rogue doctors.

The Shipman case has been seen as a repeat of the trial of Dr Adams (with whom this chapter began), who was acquitted of the murder of Mrs Morrell and died a free man in 1983. His was the first euthanasia 'show trial', and the concept of palliative care was given legitimacy during the trial. He was nicknamed 'Dr Death', as Drs Kevorkian and Shipman have also been.

Shipman was a fifty-seven-year-old GP who was tried and convicted in 2000 on twenty-one charges relating to twelve patient deaths. In fact the number was estimated to be in the high 200s or over 300. Shipman was alleged to be a beneficiary to 132 wills, and the deaths occurred in the patients' home or in his surgery. In one chilling example, he saw three other patients before telling a practice nurse that a patient was dead in one of his surgery rooms. Characterised as a serial killer and a murderer, his own suicide in prison in mid-January 2004 precludes any understanding of his motives.

It is to be hoped that he has not done irreparable damage to the matter of voluntary euthanasia and physician-assisted suicide for it is clear that his aberrant career was not inspired by any desire to assist these causes.

Notes

1. P. Singer, *Rethinking Life and Death* (Melbourne: Text, 1994), p. 69.
2. Dame Cicely Saunders, 'From the UK', *Palliative Medicine* 17 (2003).
3. Singer, *Rethinking Life and Death*, p. 67.
4. Ibid., p. 58.
5. D. T. Wade, 'Ethical Issues in Diagnosis and Management of Patients in the Permanent Vegetative State', *British Medical Journal* Vol. 322, No. 7282 (2001).
6. Singer, *Rethinking Life and Death*, p. 66.
7. Ibid.
8. J. Harris, 'Consent and End of Life Decisions', *Journal of Medical Ethics* Vol. 29, No. 1 (2003): 13.
9. R. Campbell, 'Life, Death and the Law', in *Introducing Applied Ethics*, ed. Brenda Almond (Oxford: Blackwell, 1995).
10. Ibid., p. 201.
11. Ibid., p. 202.
12. M. Cosic, *The Right to Die?* (Melbourne: New Holland Publishers, 2003), p. 151.
13. M. A. Sanderson, 'European Convention on Human Rights-Assisted Suicide: Pretty v. UK', *American Journal of International Law* (2002).
14. B. Diamond, 'Should Diane Pretty's Husband be Allowed to Help Her to Die?', *British Journal of Nursing* Vol. 11, No. 9 (2002).
15. R. Nicholson, 'Death is the Remedy?', *Hastings Center Report* Vol. 32, No. 1 (2002).

16. Sanderson, 'European Convention on Human Rights-Assisted Suicide: Pretty v. UK', p. 94.
17. R. Huxtable and A. V. Campbell, 'Palliative Care and the Euthanasia Debate: Recent Developments', *Palliative Medicine* Vol. 17 (2003).
18. Sanderson, 'European Convention on Human Rights-Assisted Suicide: Pretty v. UK'.
19. W. Hoge, 'Paralysed Woman Has Right to Die: A British Judge Rules', *New York Times*, 23 March 2002.
20. L. Doyal and L. Doyal, 'Why Active Euthanasia and Physician-Assisted Suicide Should be Legalised', *British Medical Journal* Vol. 323, No. 10 (November 2001): 1080.
21. M. Warnock, 'I Made a Bad Law – We Should Help the Ill to Die', *Sunday Times*, December 2003.
22. Karen Birchard, 'Serial Killer Doctor Sparks Calls for Legislation Changes', *Medical Post* Vol 39, No. 29 (2003); C. Dyer, 'Public Inquiry Hears How Shipman Killed Patients with Diamorphine', *BMJ*, Vol. 323 (2001); O. Dyer, 'Shipman Murdered More than 200 Patients, Inquiry Ends', *British Medical Journal* Vol. 325, No. 7357 (2000); M. Fitzpatrick, 'Auditing Deaths', *The Lancet* Vol. 362 (2003); H. G. Kinnell, 'Serial Homicide by Doctors: Shipman in Perspective', *BMJ* Vol. 321 (2000); C. Richmond, 'Medical Murders Shock England', *Canadian Medical Association Journal* Vol. 163, No. 5 (2000).

5

Legalising Euthanasia in The Netherlands

The Netherlands is a very important case study, as it represents the only country that can be seen as a test case for a liberal regime in relation to euthanasia, and in particular, voluntary euthanasia and physician-assisted suicide. Until recently it was the only country that legalised euthanasia (it was joined by Belgium in 2001). In Australia, the Northern Territory state legalised euthanasia in 1996 but was overridden by the Commonwealth nine months later, in 1997. In the US, the state of Oregon introduced the Death with Dignity Act, which came into effect in 1997 and survived a federal challenge in 2001. Both these examples are of state jurisdictions.

Significantly, the Dutch legislation in 2001 had been preceded by nearly three decades of practice where euthanasia was in effect legal, in the sense that doctors were assured they would not be prosecuted provided they followed approved guidelines. This experience makes it the only country that can provide long-term empirical data that can confirm or deny trends alleged by both advocates and opponents of euthanasia.

The Dutch scene

The candour and transparency with which the stages of the Dutch experience have been handled are admirable and make it the most honest country to have grappled with the problem. Lest we be tempted to just apply the Dutch model, however, it is important to assess the political and cultural context, and to learn the lessons implicit in the Dutch experience, before taking it to be directly transferable to another context.

The Dutch have a tradition of tolerance. They fought for religious freedom for eighty years in the sixteenth and seventeenth centuries, and The Netherlands was a refuge for Jews, Catholics and free-thinkers, including the philosophers Baruch Spinoza and René Descartes, who fled religious opposition. Calvinism was the dominant religion, but Jews and Catholics took an active part in social and business affairs. The ethos was one of pragmatic tolerance, but this did not mean integration. In a uniquely Dutch compromise (so-called pillarisation), Dutch society was compartmentalised into Roman Catholic, Protestant and secular streams, each with its own schools, hospitals, political party, medical organisations, newspaper and media. This is reflected in the current situation of fifty religions and twenty-five political parties.

Importantly, then, there was also long-standing religious tolerance between Calvinists and Roman Catholics (especially since Vatican II), and respect for and trust in the medical profession (partly because the 'family doctor' relationship is still the norm, and because of the record of Dutch doctors in refusing to cooperate with the Nazis over the sterilisation of the Jews and euthanasia of the handicapped).[1] There is also strong support for those who prefer a secular basis for morality, centred on individual choice, autonomy and individuality. Abortion was legalised in 1969, despite opposition from the churches that it was murder of innocents, but there was little interest in euthanasia compared with the USA and England, which both had voluntary euthanasia societies in the 1930s, more than forty years before one was established in The Netherlands (1976).

This history of individualism, pragmatism and tolerance produced 'gedogen', a peculiarly Dutch compromise that allowed the professed allegiance to laws to be tempered by a flexible acceptance of instances where it is preferable to break them, which can be seen as an instinctive act of utilitarianism. On this view, if drug-taking, prostitution and euthanasia are occurring, it is better that they be in the open, where they can be regulated and any damage minimised. However, another view gained currency in the light of experience. The Dutch came to see that the dual approach of de jure prohibition and de facto toleration (still taken by other countries) was too ambiguous and arbitrary in deciding issues of choice and death, and that transparency and regulation were safer. As early as 1985, then, a codified set of rules was used to guide practice; this was monitored and reviewed until April 2002, when new and more specific legislation was introduced.

What cannot be overemphasised is that the Dutch have a universal health care system, including free nursing home care, that is one of the best in the world, so that many of the negative drivers that may be behind euthanasia requests in other countries – financial fears, and inadequate medical and palliative care – are taken out of play.[2] As well as the noted individualism, there is respect for autonomy, a natural willingness to discuss moral issues openly and a polder model of decision-making – a consensus-based form of industrial relations where employees and employers remain in negotiations until consensus is reached. This also affects the way moral debate is carried out. The Netherlands also has a consensus-based legal system[3] rather than an adversarial one, as in the other three countries that are discussed here.

All these factors have produced a humane, less polarised society, where a tolerant and socially responsible humanist approach to such issues as euthanasia is held in common, even among progressive, practising Christians. This may make The Netherlands the envy of more polarised countries. It also suggests that rigorous preconditions must be in place before its approach can be used as an object lesson or an example of best practice, and be too simply transplanted into another context, where the same background and conditions do not apply.

Early euthanasia cases

Just as in the other countries examined so far, the move to voluntary euthanasia and physician-assisted suicide began in The Netherlands with a troublesome case, which two influential practitioners, van der Maas and Leenen, both see as instrumental in paving the way for toleration of euthanasia.[4] In 1971 Dr Geertruida Postma was charged with murder under Article 293 of the penal code, after she injected her mother with a dose of morphine. Her mother had been in a nursing home for some time, was deaf and partly paralysed after a cerebral haemorrhage, could hardly speak and was being treated for pneumonia. She had unsuccessfully attempted suicide and had begged her daughter for help. She had to be tied to a chair to prevent her falling. Dr Postma said, 'When I watched my mother, a human wreck, hanging in that chair, I couldn't stand it any more.' Her only regret was not having acted sooner. She informed the director of the nursing home of what she had done, who reported the death to the police.

The maximum penalty for murder was twelve years in jail, and in 1973 Dr Postma was found guilty, but given only a one-week suspended sentence and put on probation for a year. This suggests considerable public acceptance of her action. Letters poured in to the Ministry of Justice. Other doctors signed an open letter to the Minister, acknowledging they had committed the same crime. Opinion polls found a substantial majority of the public supported voluntary euthanasia. People in Dr Postma's village formed a Society for Voluntary Euthanasia, which in a decade had 25,000 members and now has 90,000 – bigger than any political party.

In 1976, the Royal Dutch Medical Association (KNMG) issued a statement advocating the retention of Article 293 of the penal code, but urging that doctors be permitted to administer pain-relieving drugs and withhold or withdraw futile, life-prolonging treatment, even if death resulted. This applied to a patient who was incurably ill and in the process of dying. A court should then decide whether there was a conflict of duties that justified the doctor's actions.

This defence was used in the Alkmaar case in 1984. This concerned a ninety-five-year-old patient, Mrs B, who was unable to eat or drink and had lost consciousness. She regained consciousness and pleaded with her doctor to end her suffering. The doctor discussed the request with his assistant physician and Mrs B's son, who both supported the request on the ground that her suffering was unbearable, though her condition was not terminal. The doctor was charged with mercy killing and convicted without punishment. Both the lower court and the Court of Appeals rejected his argument that he had faced an emergency situation of conflict between his legal duty not to kill and his duty to relieve his patient's suffering. The Supreme Court held that the Court of Appeals should have investigated whether the emergency situation had existed as the doctor claimed and overturned the conviction, invoking Article 40 of the penal code, which allows a defence of necessity in cases of conflicting responsibilities ('force majeure').[5]

The Rotterdam criteria

The case was sent back to the Rotterdam court for rehearing, and in 1984 the court came up with the 'Rotterdam criteria' to help guide doctors facing decisions on ending life. The government and the KNMG also published a list of conditions under which it was appropriate for doctors to administer voluntary euthanasia, and which, if followed, would not result in prosecution. The patient had to have:

- made a voluntary request;
- the request had to be well considered;
- the wish for death had to be enduring;
- the patient had to be suffering unacceptably;
- the doctor had to have consulted a second doctor, who agreed with the proposed course of action.

These guidelines did not require that the condition should be terminal, only that it be unbearable and without hope of improvement. Clearly they did not define key terms ('well considered', 'enduring', 'suffering unbearably' – in whose eyes?), and may be seen to have left loopholes. What they attempted to do was set limits and also leave room for discretion. In 1990 the KNMG and the Ministry of Justice agreed on a three-step notification procedure, incorporated in regulations under the Burial Act:[6]

- the physician would not issue a declaration of natural death, but would inform the local medical examiner of the circumstances by filling in a questionnaire;
- the medical examiner would report to the district attorney;
- the district attorney would decide whether the physician should be prosecuted.

The public prosecutor would thus decide on a case-by-case basis. These procedures have been in place since 1990, and became law in 1994.

The Dutch definition of euthanasia

It is extremely important to point out, in considering the Dutch experience, that the Dutch definition of euthanasia is a narrow one, restricted to active voluntary euthanasia. This goes back to the evolution of the Dutch debate. Since Van Den Berg's influential, *Medical Power and Medical Ethics* (1969) was published there has been a growing appreciation that the increased use of medical technology – particularly resuscitation and transplantation techniques – is the main cause of end-of-life questions, and hence the medical profession is primarily responsible for a solution.[7] But medical ethics widened, from 'etiquette for physicians' (Kater),[8] and lawyers, ethicists and theologians became involved in end-of life debates. To define which part of the broader category of medical decisions at the end of life should properly be called euthanasia was one of the core issues of the debate itself.

Leenen, an influential lawyer, insisted (in a very Millian way) that nobody but the patient could judge on the life of the patient. He also attributed an increase in patient requests to developments in health rights, which had grown in health care, mandating a legal approach springing from the will of the patient. This was reflected in Leenen's 1978 proposed definition of euthanasia as 'intentionally shortening life (including withdrawal of treatment) by someone at the request of the person involved'. He distinguished euthanasia from 'pseudo-euthanasia', such as stopping medically futile treatment or the refusal of (life-saving) treatment by a patient.

As vice-chairman of the State Committee on Euthanasia, his views presumably influenced its definition of euthanasia as 'ending a patient's life on his or her explicit request', a definition which had a stabilising effect on the debate, and clarified and standardised the definition of euthanasia. What fell outside the narrow definition of euthanasia was intentional life-shortening by omission – passive euthanasia – or euthanasia without request, whether voluntary or non-voluntary. Nor did it address the problems associated with patients such as severely handicapped newborns, patients in a persistent vegetative state, patients with Alzheimer's disease or psychiatric patients. The KNMG put out four reports on these categories of patients between 1990 and 1993.[9]

In these essentially boundary/jurisdictional debates, euthanasia could refer to direct action, indirect action, refraining from action, action with or without request from the patient.

At the General Meeting of the Royal Association of Physicians in 1970, the Chairman acknowledged 'an evolution going on in medical ethics' and the insufficiency of the principle of respect for life.

There was then consensus that euthanasia was an issue of autonomy, but 'mercy killing' was asserted in relation to incompetent patients – although the ethicist Dupuis preferred to appeal to 'supposed will' or 'best interest'.[10] Kuitert, another ethicist, resisted the narrowing of the debate by the emphasis on definitions and turning euthanasia into a matter of lawsuits, and sought a broader, morally acceptable professional standard, favouring the principle of mercy in the case of non-competent patients.[11] Leenen regarded 'without request' cases as beyond the bounds of legitimate medicine and opposed the government's proposal for one procedure for these two different end-of-life decisions. Nevertheless a joint report procedure for euthanasia, physician-assisted suicide and life-ending without request has been in effect since June 1994, despite World Medical Association opposition.[12]

The Remmelink reports

After more than a decade of de facto legalisation of euthanasia, in 1990 the Remmelink Commission, chaired by the Attorney General, was set up to investigate euthanasia practice. The Central Bureau of Statistics surveyed over 4,600 physicians. The results were published in 1991, and an English version, written by Dr Paul van der Maas, was published in 2002, after a 1996 article published in the *New England Journal of Medicine*. The report indicated that physicians occasionally (in about 0.8 per cent of deaths) terminated the lives of their patients without their consent. This was almost invariably when the patients were close to death and no longer capable of consent, and half such cases were initiated by the family. While this raised grounds for concern, the report could not show that the introduction of voluntary euthanasia had led to abuse, as both Helga Kuhse[13] and Peter Singer[14] have separately pointed out. For this inference to be warranted, one would need either two studies conducted several years apart and showing an increase in unjustified killings, or a comparison between The Netherlands and a similar country in which doctors practising voluntary euthanasia are liable to be prosecuted. Belgium's legislative change is too recent for such a study to be available, though such a comparison may be possible a decade further on.

Swarte and Heintz[15] probe the reasons for requesting euthanasia, and cite van der Maas's 1990 study that loss of dignity (fifty-seven per cent), pain (forty-six per cent), dying in an unworthy way (forty-six per cent), dependence on others (thirty-three per cent) or being tired of life (ten per cent) were predominant. In only ten of 187 cases was pain given as the single reason. This was confirmed by a 1994 study by van der Wal, who found pain was the most important reason in only five per cent of requests. Swarte and Heintz conclude that in the Dutch situation, it is clear that the main reason for requesting euthanasia or assisted suicide (EAS) is loss of dignity and dying in an unworthy way, which the patient considered unacceptable.

In 1995 there was a second Remmelink survey, which evaluated the adequacy of the notification procedures introduced in 1990 and legalised in 1994 (previously described). It did not show any significant increase in the rate of non-voluntary euthanasia, and thus empirically dispelled fears that the country was sliding down a slippery slope. Moreover, studies were carried out in Australia and Belgium,[16] to discover whether there was more abuse in The Netherlands than in other countries where euthanasia was illegal and could not be practised openly. Survey questions in the Dutch study were put to doctors concerning both direct treatment and forgoing medical treatment, such as withholding antibiotics or withdrawing artificial ventilation. The findings suggest that while the rate of active voluntary euthanasia in Australia is slightly lower than the most recent Dutch study (1.8 per cent compared to 2.3 per cent), the rate of non-voluntary euthanasia is considerably higher (3.5 per cent compared to 0.8 per cent). Other end-of-life decisions foreseen to be life-shortening were also higher than in The Netherlands.

The Belgian study came to similar conclusions. The rate of voluntary euthanasia (at 1.3 per cent of all deaths) was lower than the Dutch, but the proportion of patients given an unrequested lethal injection was (at three per cent of all deaths) similar to Australia and higher than the Dutch.

The Belgian study concluded with a reasonable suggestion:

Perhaps less attention is given to the requirement of careful end-of-life practice in a society with a restrictive approach than in one with an open approach that tolerates and regulates euthanasia and physician assisted suicide.[17]

It is in fact both possible and likely that legalising voluntary euthanasia and physician-assisted suicide makes it easier to monitor what is happening and so prevent harm to the vulnerable.

The two studies counter the suggestion that the open practice of active euthanasia in The Netherlands had caused an increase in non-voluntary euthanasia. Even more weight should be given to the fact that Belgium, The Netherlands' neighbour and closest to the Dutch debate and practice, has followed the Dutch lead.[18]

Moreover, as Kuhse points out,[19] while the Remmelink report showed the rarity of active euthanasia (2.6 per cent of all deaths) and physician-assisted suicide (0.3 per cent) of all deaths), thirty-five per cent of deaths resulted from two other kinds of medical end of life decisions, generally deemed acceptable – 17.5 per cent from withholding or withdrawing treatment, and 17.5 per cent from life-shortening palliative care. In terms of absolute numbers and scope for abuse, then, these latter categories should surely be of more concern. But we have seen in each of the countries examined that this is not so, which seems paradoxical.

Despite the pessimistic predictions, only one per cent of deaths in The Netherlands are the result of euthanasia, and two out of three requests are turned down because they do not meet the criteria. Zbigniew Zylincz, a Dutch palliative care doctor, says unofficial numbers suggest a 10–13 per cent drop in euthanasia cases, because of the legalisation on voluntary euthanasia and because of growing interest in, and availability of, palliative care.[20]

In 1991 the Chabot case[21] further pushed the boundaries, when a psychiatrist, Bourdewijn Chabot, agreed to assist a severely depressed woman to commit suicide. She was a physically fit fifty-five-year-old who had lost one son to suicide, another to cancer, and whose marriage had ended. Chabot considered her to be suffering incurable grief and agreed to provide the prescription for drugs that would end her life. He wrote to several colleagues seeking a second opinion, and the majority agreed, despite not having seen the patient. When Chabot lodged the necessary forms with the coroner and the case was reluctantly pursued, Chabot was found guilty of breaching the guidelines by not bringing in another specialist to see the woman in person.

However, this seems to reflect as badly on the other doctors as on Chabot. He was acquitted. There has been ongoing debate since over the importance of seeing patients when consultation is involved – and not just psychiatric patients. Importantly, the Dutch Supreme Court agreed that mental suffering was sufficient reason for assisting a suicide. This is important if suffering is taken to be sufficient justification, but is also clearly grist to the mill of anti-euthanasia advocates who invoke slippery slope arguments.

The governing Christian Democrats (with a Roman Catholic leader, Prime Minister Ruud Lubbers) feared they were embarking on a slippery slope, which might come to encompass the mentally ill or the depressed.

They came under increasing pressure from the opposition and from their coalition partners, the Social Democrats, to decriminalise voluntary euthanasia further. In 1993 the lower house of the Dutch Parliament passed the Termination of Life on Request and Assisted Suicide (Review) Procedures Act by 91 to 45. The margin was narrower in the upper house because the small parties there saw it as 'a spineless compromise' and urged full legalisation. Even some Roman Catholic parliamentarians voted for it, despite the Vatican injunction against voluntary euthanasia, because it gave the state prosecutor a means to control existing practice.

In 1994 the Christian Democrats lost power to the Social Democrats, in coalition with D66, a social liberal party, and VDD, a conservative liberal party. The debate was reopened, but was not a top priority during the first coalition term of office (1994 – 98), when D66 presented a Bill on its own in 1998, just prior to fresh elections.

At the time this debate was taking place, an eighty-six-year-old former senator Edward Brongersma committed suicide with the assistance of Doctor Philip Sutorius.[22] He too did not have a terminal illness, but was suffering from incontinence, dizziness, immobility and was 'tired of life'. Dr Sutorius was charged with assisting suicide in what was expected to be a test case that would set limits on acceptable euthanasia. The Haarlem High Court found he had fulfilled the legal guidelines and acquitted him. In December 2001 the Amsterdam Appeal Court found him guilty because he did not act for medical reasons, but did not impose a sentence because he acted out of compassion for his patient – and the court saw it as a test case for the prosecutor.

Further euthanasia legislation was presented in the second term of the coalition government. It took voluntary euthanasia away from the jurisdiction of the state prosecutor; it also allowed minors over the age of twelve to make their own decision about euthanasia, without parental consent. This was amended during debate to require parental agreement for children between twelve and sixteen, and parental involvement between sixteen and eighteen. Here many would think the Dutch have gone too far. This would still be far too radical for many people, and in fact departs from Mill's criterion of adulthood.

Both the inclusion of mental suffering and the extension to juveniles may seem so abhorrent that for some this damns the whole approach. If this is the community standard, it would be possible to insist, in guidelines, regulations or legislation, that only adults were eligible – perhaps on the Millian ground that the whole autonomy argument applies only to 'human beings in the maturity of their faculties, not children or young persons below the age which the law may fix as that of manhood or womanhood'.

This may seem stipulative or arbitrary, but is so for good reason. More is at stake here than settling on a driving age. Whether the scope should be confined to physical suffering and terminal suffering is perhaps a harder question.

Why prioritise physical suffering? Is it because we can argue it is terminal? Is it because it is a safer standard? As Singer has argued,[23] suffering is suffering. The condition invoked is 'unbearable'. Safeguards would need to be invoked, such as psychiatric assessment. That two out of three requests are rejected suggests compliance is not automatic. I personally would prefer the scope to be limited on both these points. The arguments concerning physical suffering seem more convincing. Clearly too, if death is imminent, in relieving the physical suffering we are only anticipating what would surely follow. This seems a lesser evil than bringing about an outcome which would otherwise not have occurred, and our responsibility seems commensurably lessened.

There is also the pragmatic argument, which is to go with what consensus can be achieved and see what experience and the community response are. Experience may prove reassuring, and further steps may be possible later.

As it stood, the Dutch legislation was both clear and comprehensive. It was passed in April 2002, with the support of an astonishing ninety-two per cent of the population and ninety-two per cent of the media.[24] It elaborates the 'due care' requirements of the 1991 regulations and takes oversight of the procedure out of the hands of the police prosecutor. Assisting someone to die remains an offence within the penal code, but can be overridden by the defence of necessity ('force majeure'). The new law also recognises the legal basis for advance directives even if a patient is unable to signify his or her wishes at the time.

Five regional committees have been established since the end of 1998 to decide whether doctors carrying out euthanasia have complied with the 1993 guidelines. Under the 2001 law, the doctor still reports to the regional committee (a lawyer, a doctor and an ethicist), but the committee now only reports breaches to the prosecutor's office. The burden of proof has thus been changed, from the onus being on the doctors to prove they had followed guidelines to the regional committees to prove guilt. Much of the responsibility has been devolved, and eighty per cent of the people are in favour of the law and the current practice.

Somerville emphasises this change in the burden of proof.[25] She characterises the effect of the legislation as moving the Dutch from a 'no' prima facie presumption in theory and a 'yes, but' or possibly a 'no' presumption in practice, to a clearly 'yes, but' presumption. She outlines four possible presumptions:

- 'no' (euthanasia should be prohibited);
- 'no, unless' (there is a basic presumption against euthanasia unless conditions are fulfilled, but it should be allowed in some circumstances);
- 'yes, but' (euthanasia should be allowed in general, but prohibited in some circumstances);
- 'yes' (euthanasia should be allowed).

This is an unusual and interesting classification, the 'no, unless' suggestion being because the legal justification for euthanasia was, as we have seen in the Alkmaar case, the defence of 'force majeure' or conflicting duties, which excused something that would otherwise be prohibited.

A third Remmelink report came out in May 2003, and an abbreviated copy was published in *The Lancet* in June 2003.[26] There is no English version, but the UK Voluntary Euthanasia

Society published an English translation of the executive summary. (Importantly, the data are for 2001, and do not reflect experience under the new laws, which came into effect in April 2002.)

Key findings of the report were that there is no empirical support for the supposition that The Netherlands is 'going downhill' in relation to life-terminating treatment by physicians, and the rate of voluntary euthanasia and assisted suicide and the practice of medical decision-making relating to the end of life in The Netherlands appear to have stabilised.

Both life-terminating treatment on request and without request are no more frequent than they were six years ago. In 2001, the number of cases of euthanasia was 3,500 – 2.5 per cent of all deaths. Assisted suicide cases are estimated at 300 – 0.2 per cent of all deaths, compared to the two previous studies, where the figure was 0.3 per cent (in both studies). The total percentage of cases of euthanasia and assisted suicide in 2001–2 seems effectively unaltered from 1995–6 at 2.7 per cent, and were mainly performed by family physicians, who frequently care for patients dying at home.

Importantly, the 2001–2 report contained a new section on the correlation between socio-economic status and medical decisions concerning the end of life. It found no signs indicating an increase in life-terminating treatment among vulnerable patient groups. Non-treatment decisions and euthanasia were slightly more frequent in the group with the highest socio-economic status.

As in previous investigations, life-terminating treatment 'occurs relatively little' among the elderly and people in care. Eighty-five per cent of cases of euthanasia occur in people with cancer, most frequently in the 50–60 year age group.

'Tired of life' requests occurred 5–15 times a year and seldom among children – 0.7 per cent for cases of death in the 1–16 year age group, and mainly related to cancer. Euthanasia among dementia patients was so low that an estimate of annual cases was not available. The authors, van der Wal and van der Maas, wrote:

> It is a reasonable assumption that if it happens, it is almost always a question of serious suffering as a result of an additional condition, and that euthanasia because of dementia alone effectively never happens.[27]

Inadequate palliative care was not a factor in decisions to end life, there was no difference in treatment of patients who had or had not made a request, and ninety per cent of relations of patients for whom euthanasia was implemented considered adequate care was provided in the final stages of life.

In five per cent of all death cases, terminal sedation was used, in twenty-one per cent of these, with the explicit intention of ending life.

Reporting rates had also improved, with fifty per cent of cases of euthanasia and assisted suicide reported to a Regional Review Committee, compared to forty-one per cent of 1995. The greatest increase was among general practitioners. Improvement in turnaround time of processing such cases in the Regional Review Committees is thought to have contributed to the increased willingness to report cases. Significantly – and surprisingly – physicians reported more often in 2001–2 that they had become more restrictive about euthanasia than in previous years, and less often that they had become more permissive.

Decisions to withhold or withdraw potentially life-saving treatment were most frequently made for elderly patients, with a higher frequency among female patients – explained by the fact that women generally die later than men. Alleviation of pain while taking into account or appreciating a life-shortening effect, occurred in about twenty per cent of cases in all age groups. The practice was more frequent among female than male patients, frequently involved cancer patients and was most commonly practised by home physicians. The practice increased most among people aged eighty years and older and among patients with diseases other than cancer. While other end-of-life decisions frequently involved cancer, non-treatment decisions commonly involved other diagnoses as well.[28]

In summary, euthanasia remains mainly restricted to groups other than patients with cancer, younger than eighty years and cared for by family physicians, who were frequently involved in 1990.[29] The rate of physician-assisted suicide remains low compared to that for euthanasia, despite the recommendation of the KNMG to choose physician-assisted suicide if possible.

The authors expressed surprise at the absence of a rise in the non-treatment decisions after 1995, but expressed confidence in the high participation rates and coherence of data between different studies and different years, grounding their confidence that 'our findings are a reliable overview of end-of-life decision-making practice in Holland'. They point to a growing awareness that end-of-life care should aim at improving the quality of life of patients and their families, through prevention and relief of pain and symptoms.

Swarte and Heintz attributed the minor increase in EAS (euthanasia and assisted suicide) to the careful way it is practised by physicians in The Netherlands. They point out that one of the major concerns with EAS is family pressure on the patient because of financial reasons, and that this is not an issue in The Netherlands, where every patient has health care insurance, private or national, and warn that it is not advisable to introduce EAS into countries where medical care is not – or not sufficiently – covered by insurance. A similar warning was given by Professor John Legeemaate when the legislation was passed. He pointed out to the *Guardian* newspaper three key characteristics of Dutch society: a tendency to be open; a long-term relationship with their GP; and the fact that nursing home care is free, so there are no economic pressures towards shortening life;[30]

> If you have a country in which one or more of these elements is lacking, you should be very cautious.

This warning can hardly be over-stressed. Shannon's critique of America (below) can be applied to England and Australia: certainly none of the other countries examined here can match the Dutch record in these respects.

> While the United States has an excellent system of rescue medicine, the track record on end-of-life care is rather poor. We seem willing to spend millions to delay or prolong death using the most sophisticated medical technologies, but unwilling to put money into hospice care or even appropriate training for pain management. The question of euthanasia and PAS does not stand alone; it is part of a larger discussion of the provision of health care in this country, a debate we continue to avoid.[31]

Another point to emphasise, arising out of the Dutch experience, is a pragmatic one: the desirability of following the Dutch practice in terms of definitions of euthanasia and physician-assisted suicide – and even lumping them together as EAS.[32] As we have seen, the Dutch went through the same definitional and conceptual problems as other jurisdictions, but settled on a definition which, though narrow, enabled them to conduct three major studies that are consistent and comparable. Moreover, the study design and questions have been adopted in two other international studies, which opened the door for international consistency and comparability.[33] Materstvedt and Kaasa quote the view of Paul van der Maas, author of the key Dutch studies, that international standards for comparison are badly needed across cultures and times.

The Dutch have clearly been the trendsetters in this area, conducting their experiment in a virtual gold-fish bowl for thirty years, and so have set a precedent that other jurisdictions would do well to follow, rather than to reinvent the wheel and adopt other approaches, which are then not directly comparable.

Differences of opinion about palliative care, about consultation[34] and about unreported cases remain.[35] There is a recognised need for training in pain management and palliative care, which is being addressed by courses given by Zbigniew Zylicz, including a one-day course in palliative care for twenty physicians (booked out a year in advance), plus a three-day basic course for nursing home physicians and an advanced course for thirty-five.

There is also the SCEN initiative. In 1997 the Support and Consultation of Euthanasia in Amsterdam (SCEA) unit was established, involving twenty GPs, acting as consultants to physicians, who were required to consult one of them before performing euthanasia. The participating GPs filled in a requisition form for each time they were consulted. In all, 109 consultations took place between 1997 and 1998. Three focus groups were held a year later, and then a full evaluation, suggesting more attention to palliative care. Doctors were trained to be alert to any family pressure, and the rise in reporting rates has been attributed to this project.

SCEA became a national project (SCEN), and has had a positive effect in both consulting and reporting. It may well prove more effective in shaping Dutch practice than any legal regulation, and shows a commendable willingness to address any problem areas and to try a multi-pronged approach.[36]

There is a large literature, and there has been a lot of public scrutiny over three decades. In that sense, the Dutch experience has been a 'warts and all' one, from which others can learn.

The body of Remmelink reports is unique and presents vital empirical evidence, conducted at three stages over a decade, which should assist in allaying doubts, fears and scepticism. It reveals an admirable resolve to unearth the facts concerning voluntary euthanasia and assisted suicide.

Olde Rikkert calls the Dutch government courageous and far-sighted for funding such studies, at the risk of being called 'the European Oregon'.[37] (Oregon was influenced by the Dutch model, and its experiences have had a reciprocal influence on The Netherlands.)

In terms of scrutiny and a staged response – medical association guidelines (1976), medical association and government guidelines (1984), notification procedures (1990), government reports (1990, 1995 and 2003), legislation (1993 and 2002), review committees (1998 and 2002) – the process of the Dutch experience seems close to exemplary. Its practice and evolution have been a talking point for three decades, and it has been an influential model for other jurisdictions. Most of all, it has been a model in that it has managed to progress, carefully and conscientiously, and in stages, without polarising the country – a truly enviable and unique achievement.

Notes

1. R. Cohen-Almagor, 'Why the Netherlands?', *Journal of Law, Medicine and Ethics* Vol. 30, No. 1 (2002).
2. N. B. Swarte and A. P. M. Heintz, 'Guidelines for an Acceptable Euthanasia Procedure', *Best Practice and Research Clinical Anaesthesiology* Vol. 15, No. 20 (2001).
3. H. Hendin, 'The Dutch Experience', *Issues in Law and Medicine* Vol. 17, No. 3 (2003).
4. Swarte and Heintz, 'Guidelines for an Acceptable Euthanasia Procedure'; L. J. Materstvedt and S. Kaasa, 'Euthanasia and Physician-Assisted Suicide in Scandanavia', *Palliative Medicine* (2002).
5. Hendin, 'The Dutch Experience'.
6. I. Haverkate et al., 'Guidelines on Euthanasia and Pain Alleviation: Compliance and Opinions of Physicians', *Health Policy* Vol. 44 (1998).
7. H. ten Have, 'Euthanasia: Moral Paradoxes', *Palliative Medicine* (2001).
8. L. Kater et al., 'Health Care Ethics and Health Law in the Dutch

Discussion on End-of-Life Decisions: A Historical Analysis of the Dynamics and Development of Both Disciplines', *Studies in History and Philosophy of Biological and Biomedical Sciences* Vol. 34 (2003).

9. J. van Holsteyn and M. Trappenburg, 'Citizens' Opinions on New Form of Euthanasia: A Report from the Netherlands', *Patient Education and Counselling* (1998).

10. Kater et al., 'Health Care Ethics and Health Law in the Dutch Discussion on End-of-Life Decisions'.

11. Ibid.

12. V. English et al., 'Legislation on Euthanasia', *Journal of Medical Ethics* Vol. 27 (2001).

13. H. Kuhse, 'Accepting Responsibility: Dying in Australia and the Netherlands', in *Willing to Listen, Wanting to Die*, ed. H. Kuhse (Harmondsworth: Penguin, 1994).

14. P. Singer, 'Voluntary Euthanasia: A Utilitarian Perspective', *Bioethics* Vol. 17, Nos. 5–6 (2001).

15. Swarte and Heintz, 'Guidelines for an Acceptable Euthanasia Procedure'.

16. J. J. van Delden, 'Slippery Slopes in Flat Countries – a Response', *Journal of Medical Ethics* Vol. 25 (1999).

17. Luc Deliens et al., 'End-of-Life Decisions in Medical Practice in Flanders, Belgium: A Nationwide Survey', *The Lancet* Vol. 356, No. 25 (November 2000).

18. L. Deliens and G. van der Waal, 'The Euthanasia Laws in Belgium and the Netherlands', *The Lancet* Vol. 362 (2003).

19. Kuhse, 'Accepting Responsibility: Dying in Australia and the Netherlands'.

20. M. Cosic, *The Right to Die?* (Melbourne: New Holland Publishers, 2003), p. 219.

21. Materstvedt and Kaasa, 'Euthanasia and Physician-Assisted Suicide in Scandinavia'.

22. Sheldon, 'Dutch GP Cleared after Helping to End Man's "Hopeless Existence"', and Sheldon, 'Being "Tired of Life" is not Grounds for Euthanasia'.

23. Singer, 'Voluntary Euthanasia: A Utilitarian Perspective'.

24. R. Cohen-Almagor, 'Culture of Death in the Netherlands: Dutch Perspectives', *Issues in Law and Medicine* Vol. 17, No. 2 (2001).

25. Somerville, *Death Talk*.

26. B. D. Onwuteaka-Philipsen et al., 'Euthanasia and Other End-of-Life Decisions in the Netherlands in 1990, 1995 and 2001', *The Lancet* Vol. 362 (2003).

27. Ibid.

28. Ibid.

29. Deliens and van der Waal, 'The Euthanasia Laws in Belgium and the Netherlands'.

30. Cosic, *The Right to Die?*, p. 223.

31. T. A. Shannon, 'Killing Them Softly with Kindness: Euthanasia Legislation in the Netherlands', *America* Vol. 185, No. 11 (2001): 18.
32. Swarte and Heintz, 'Guidelines for an Acceptable Euthanasia Procedure'.
33. ten Have, 'Euthanasia: Moral Paradoxes'.
34. M. Banninck et al., 'Psychiatric Consultation and Quality of Decision Making in Euthanasia', *The Lancet* Vol. 356, No. 16 (December 2000); L. Onwuteaka-Philipsen and G. van der Wal, 'A Protocol for Consulting Another Physician in Cases of Euthanasia and Assisted Suicide', *Journal of Medical Ethics* Vol. 22, No. 8 (2001).
35. Birchard, 'Serial Killer Doctor Sparks Calls for Legislation Changes'.
36. Cohen-Almagor, 'Culture of Death in the Netherlands: Dutch Perspectives'; N. G. Finlay and B. van Dijk, 'Euthanasia: The Dutch Experience and What it Entails in Practice', *The Lancet Oncology* Vol. 3, March (2002); F. van Kolfschooten, 'Dutch Television Report Stirs up Euthanasia Controversy', *The Lancet* Vol. 361 (2003).
37. M. G. M. O. Rikkert and W. H. L. Hoefnagels, 'Nutrition in the Terminal Stages of Life in Nursing-Home Patients', *Age and Ageing* Vol. 30 (2001).

6

A Legislative Experiment in Australia

Australia is the only country in the world that fully occupies a continent. As a former British colony, its government and institutions are modelled on the Westminster system, with government split between a federal government, six states and two territories, the Northern Territory and the ACT, site of the national capital, Canberra. Unlike the states, the territories are not fully self-governing and can have their legislation overruled by the Commonwealth of Australia. This is highly salient in the context of euthanasia in Australia.

This demarcation became particularly relevant in the Northern Territory, where the Rights of the Terminally Ill Act[1] permitting voluntary euthanasia was passed in 1996, but was overturned nine months later by federal parliament in 1997 with the Euthanasia Laws Act. The Northern Territory Act had been preceded by a review of the Natural Death Act 1987. At that time, Northern Territory legislation did not protect a patient's right to refuse unwanted medical treatment, nor protect doctors by permitting a defence of 'double effect' if they gave pain relief that hastened death.

For a brief period, the Northern Territory was the only jurisdiction in the world that permitted euthanasia, for The Netherlands at that time retained the prohibition in law, while following a de facto practice of permission, provided guidelines were followed (see chapter 5). In the American state of Oregon, legalised physician-assisted suicide was confirmed in November 1997.

Withdrawal of treatment – John McEwan to Mrs V

As was the case in America and England, some of Australia's early high-profile cases involved withdrawal of treatment, perhaps the most straightforward dilemmas of choice and death.

John McEwan[2]

John McEwan, a young man in his twenties, dived into the Murray River at Echuca in Victoria in January 1988 and broke his neck. He became a paraplegic, unable to use any of his muscles from the neck down. He could breathe on his own for just a few hours, then needed a ventilator. He wanted the ventilator withdrawn. When it was not, he refused to eat and was declared insane – which would have allowed force-feeding. This was rescinded when he agreed to eat and to take anti-depressants. Still at times he refused food and medication, and frequently expressed the wish to die by having treatment withdrawn. After twelve months in hospital he returned home, to 24-hour nursing care and care from his GP and physician, Dr Toscano. He still wanted withdrawal of treatment. The case attracted considerable media attention, state MPs were contacted and public opinion was strongly on his side.

On 3 April 1986, he was found dead with the respirator disconnected. A coroner's inquiry found he had died of cardiac respiratory arrest. Dr Toscano believed John should not have been kept alive against his will, but had continued treatment because he had received legal advice to do so and could otherwise have faced a charge of manslaughter. Other legal opinion disagreed. Clearly the law needed clarification.

Mrs N[3]

Mrs N, a forty-year-old married mother of two, was admitted to St Vincent's Hospital in Melbourne in 1988 with breathing difficulties, and was put on a ventilator. She was diagnosed with motor neurone disease, a terminal condition. Mrs N wanted the ventilator withdrawn, which would lead to her death. Nicholas Tonti-Filippini the hospital ethicist, was consulted. The ventilator was turned down, the oxygen level was increased and, after six hours of consciousness, Mrs N died in the seventh hour from carbon dioxide retention. Motor neurone disease was declared the underlying cause of death. A press conference was held, and there was no legal challenge.

However some months later Tonti-Filippini was provocatively introduced as a speaker as coming 'fresh from the killing fields of St Vincent's' and challenged by Jana Wendt, a reporter on the television show 'A Current Affair', with the fact that some people regarded him as a murderer.

Later that year, the Medical Treatment Act was passed in Victoria, which provided that competent patients who were not suicidal have the right to refuse medical treatment, including life-sustaining treatment, and protected doctors who implement the patient's request. Similar legislation was passed in all states. Until then, doctors were caught between the law of negligence if they did not provide treatment and the law of trespass if they continued treatment. Both John McEwan and Mrs N refused burdensome treatment. Tonti-Filippini endorsed this, though he found deliberately shortening of human life always morally wrong.[4] He was at the time of these two cases the only hospital ethicist in Australia, and St Vincent's was the only hospital in Australia with an ethics research facility. St Vincent's was, and is, a Roman Catholic hospital with a strong moral tradition, a reputation for conservatism and strong public trust. Had the action taken over Mrs N happened elsewhere, there may well have been more of a furore.

Mrs V

In 2003 the Victorian Supreme Court case of Gardner; re B WV[5] was an even more complex case concerning withdrawal of medical treatment, for this case involved the Public Advocate and whether the provision of nutrition and hydration by artificial means constitutes palliative care or medical treatment. Mrs V was a sixty-eight-year-old woman suffering from Pick's disease, a form of dementia, who had been in foetal position and had had no cortical activity for three years, though her brain stem functioned normally. She was receiving fluid and nutrition via percutaneous endoscopic gastronomy (PEG) feeding. The Advocate sought to have PEG feeding declared medical treatment, which could be refused, rather than palliative care, which could not. Catholic Health Australia Incorporated and the Right to Life Association were both given leave to appear as amicus curiae rather than as a party.

Mrs V had begged her husband to spare her a slow, painful death, and had expressed this to him while she was still able to communicate. She had not signed an advance health directive.

The case arose because the Medical Treatment Act 1988[6] had clarified the law relating to the right of patients to refuse medical treatment. This was subsequently amended in 1990 to enable an agent or guardian to make decisions about medical treatment on behalf of an incompetent patient. This case was the first legal test of that amendment.

The issues were whether medical treatment did include palliative care and whether palliative care included 'reasonable provision of food and water' but did not include artificial feeding.

Mrs V's family had approached Dr Rodney Syme, of the Voluntary Euthanasia Association, for help in 2002, which had led to the approach to the Public Advocate. The Public Advocate's barrister argued that the case was not about euthanasia or mercy killing, but about withdrawal of treatment. The Roman Catholic church and the Right to Life Association argued that Mrs V's death was not imminent and that the purpose of withdrawal of treatment was to end her life, which would follow within one to four weeks of withdrawal of treatment.

The Tony Bland case (see chapter 5) was an important precedent in the case. Justice Morris quoted both Hoffman LJ and Lord Goff – Hoffman for noting a cluster of ethical principles (sanctity of life, individual autonomy, respect for the dignity of the individual human being), while noting that there is no morally correct solution, and that accommodation is necessary between principles which have come into conflict with one another. From Lord Goff Justice Morris took the comparison of artificial feeding being analogous to a ventilator in the case of Tony Bland:

> Anthony is not merely incapable of feeding himself. He is incapable of swallowing, and therefore of eating or drinking in the normal sense of those words. There is overwhelming evidence that, in the medical profession, artificial treatment is regarded as a form of medical treatment, and even if it is not medical treatment it must form part of the medical care of the patient. Indeed, the function of

artificial feeding in the case of Anthony, by means of a nasogastric tube, is to provide a form of life support analogous to that provided by a ventilator, which artificially breathes air in and out of the lungs of a patient incapable of breathing normally, thereby enabling oxygen to reach the bloodstream.[7]

Suicide, assisted suicide and voluntary euthanasia

Cornelius Hus[8]

The 1986 case of Cornelius Hus and Wayne MacDonald and the 1993 case of Chris Hill have some parallels with that of John McEwan, but here the issue was assisted suicide. Cornelius Hus was a twenty-two-year-old who became a quadriplegic after a motorcycle accident. He and his friend Wayne MacDonald had met in primary school, hanging out in Geelong and becoming 'blood brothers' in their teens. After ten months in hospital, Cornelius came home. His father had built him a bungalow and a high concrete wall to shelter him from the sight of the swimming pool across the road. In hospital he had not wanted to live, but the lethal injection his parents had requested was not legally available. He hoped he would regain enough movement in his hand to shoot himself, but never did. He became increasingly desperate. On 21 July 1985 Wayne MacDonald shot his friend in the head, then shot himself – whether because he was scared of the legal aftermath of what he had done, or in a murder–suicide pact that was a tragic expression of 'mateship'. The deaths received a lot of media attention. Channel Nine's 'Willesee Programme' paid for both funerals in return for exclusive interviews with the Hus family. This was a rare case of voluntary euthanasia by a friend rather than a family member. Both mothers now fight for voluntary euthanasia laws.

Once again there is the same pattern as in America, England and The Netherlands, of hard-won gains and progress being made only in the wake of anguishing personal cases and considerable media pressure.

Chris Hill[9]

Chris Hill exemplifies this pattern. A journalist on the *Australian Geographic* magazine, he became paralysed from the chest down after a hang-gliding accident in February 1992. In April 1993, after fourteen months of struggling to cope with his situation, he took his own life in his car, in a remote car park, after leaving a letter to his family, friends and colleagues celebrating his life before the accident, seeing death as a release and expressing bitterness about not being given the choice of a dignified death.

His doctor described him as 'the best-rehabilitated paraplegic I had ever met', yet understood it was not enough. He deplored the fact that Chris was denied any assistance with 'the most important act of his life', saying his family should have been with him, in some warm comforting place, and that 'the strident voices who "sanctify life" drove him to an unpleasant death'.

Other heart-rending, anonymous accounts in Helga Kuhse's *Willing to Listen, Wanting to Die* chronicle the ten-year anniversary of a daughter giving tablets to her mother but having finally to use a pillow, a medical practitioner administering medication to her husband and also having to use a pillow, a nurse assisting her husband with a morphine injection, and needing to resort to a plastic bag, and a wife administering tablets to her husband – all burdened by what they had to do, all fearful of the consequences and all insisting there must be a better way. Steve J. Spears, the author of the play *The Elocution of Benjamin Franklin*, writes bitterly of his mother's death from cancer in 1988, and her wish to die before the cancer reached her brain and while she was still sane – a wish that could not be fulfilled because she could not ask her doctor to help her die with dignity with a dose of narcotics. Spears includes copies of his letters to the then prime minister and state premiers, and their formal and perfunctory replies reaffirming the law in relation to voluntary euthanasia.

Pressure was clearly building in Australia, as in other countries, and in 1994 the Australian Medical Association surveyed its members. Half said they had been asked to hasten death, and twenty-eight per cent had agreed. Fifty per cent of doctors replied affirmatively to the question: 'If active voluntary euthanasia were legal, and an incurably ill patient asked you to hasten death, would you comply with that request?' However, the Australian Medical Association remains staunchly opposed.

Voluntary euthanasia and physician-assisted suicide

In 1995, led by Dr Rodney Syme, seven doctors signed an open letter[10] addressed to the Victorian Premier, which was published in *The Age* newspaper. They argued for the legalisation of voluntary euthanasia at the individual's request to end unbearable suffering, on the ground that it would be regulating a practice that was already widespread, but in a covert, discretionary way. Dr Syme described his journey 'from innocent to advocate' in Helga Kuhse's *Willing to Listen, Wanting to Die*[11] (already cited), and his sense of helplessness, impotence, shame and guilt at being unable to assist a fifty-two-year-old woman with cancer in 1972. He also described having to lie to avoid a possible fourteen-year jail sentence for assisting suicide after he prescribed sleeping tablets for a seventy-five-year-old widower with bladder cancer, and administering morphine to a close relative in 1976.

In 1991, he was contacted by the daughter of a fifty-year-old man, who was seeking help for her father to end his life. Suffering from a progressive neurological disease, he had already been resuscitated against his will two years earlier, after swallowing heroin tablets. His wife panicked when he had not died some hours later and called the local doctor, who had him taken by ambulance to the local public hospital, where he was resuscitated despite his wife holding a medical power of attorney under the Victorian Medical Treatment Act and her assurance that he did not want to be resuscitated. Dr Syme commented that the Labor Government of the day and the subsequent Liberal Government had done very little to promulgate the legislation.

Dr Syme was called by the man, who now could not leave the house and could find no other doctor to visit him. While drawing the line at prescribing lethal drugs, Dr Syme assured him that if he attempted a drug overdose, he would be admitted to hospital under Dr Syme's care and no resuscitation or life-prolonging measures would be undertaken. Three months later, that is what occurred.

Dr Syme expressed regret at breaking the law, a wish for a colleague's opinion and the ability to have prescribed medication that would act more quickly than sixty hours, but no regret for his action. To have acted otherwise would have been immoral:

> Is it not ironic that an animal in the same condition as that unfortunate man would be granted more compassion and dignity by our society than was this helpless human being, and others like him? Is it not time for society to listen to the anguish of those who reasonably want to die?[12]

Indeed, it surely is.

Dr Syme, now president of the Voluntary Euthanasia Society of Victoria, however, prefers assisted suicide to voluntary euthanasia in the sense of lethal injection administered by a doctor. Not only is it the patient's responsibility, but it is a safer method in that there is less room for error in communication. He has tested the law by not hiding his intentions on death certificates – not fudging the issue by putting 'cardiac arrest'. He has reported cases to the Victorian coroner three times, demanding a workable definition of the double-effect doctrine and clarification of his position as a doctor.[13] In 1975 he wrote to the Victoria coroner asking whether it was necessary to report a death due to terminal sedation – a method he describes as lacking dignity for the patient and gruelling for the family, and not a natural death, though such cases were not reported to the coroner. The letter of reply was unsatisfactory, and though his letter was referred to the Attorney General who agreed there was a case for reporting such cases, the matter was left at that.

In 1997 Dr Syme reported the death of a woman to the coroner and requested an inquest under the Coroner's Act. In telling his story, he was trying to force the issue, and the matter was referred to the College of Physicians, who took an opinion from a palliative care specialist, who criticised his practice in detail, but not in principle, so the coroner decided the treatment was acceptable and the matter was not reportable. However it took four years from the woman's death to the coroner's final reply!

Dr Syme put two further cases before the coroner. One was of a woman with multiple sclerosis, in a nursing home, whose only option was to refuse food and water. The patient was moved to a private hospital and signed a refusal of treatment form. After forty-eight hours, Dr Syme gave her sedation and she died seven days later. This case took two and a half years to resolve. Unlike the first woman, this woman was not suffering from a terminal illness and could have lived a further several years.

Dr Syme reported a third case to the coroner before receiving any verdict on the previous two. This was a man with advanced skin cancer and brain tumours. He had decided to refuse food and water, but his palliative care providers would not sedate him. Dr Syme again moved the man to a private hospital where he died under sedation in two days. Without sedation, Dr Syme said, he would have 'struggled to dehydrate to death in a conscious state – which is pretty barbaric'.

When this case was reported to the coroner, an assistant rang and said there was no need to report the death as the coroner had accepted that the death was due to melanoma and that that should be signed on the death certificate. Dr Syme would not sign the certificate, which was eventually signed by the coroner's pathologist. The coroner eventually decided the death was not reportable. The 'crazy' (according to Dr Syme) upshot is that this intentional form of hastening death can be practised with impunity, without regulation. It is effectively a form of voluntary euthanasia that is available and not widely known by the medical community or the wider public. This is not good policy, nor good practice, requiring a series of case-by-case reports, seeking definition and clarification, and remaining a matter of communication between Dr Syme and the coroner, despite his efforts to bring it to wider attention.

What this saga shows is a sustained campaign by a brave doctor determined to bring the issue into the open and end the subterfuge and evasion that were the status quo.

In each country, it takes a crusading doctor to force the issue and push the boundaries. In the case of Australia, there is the paradox of 80 per cent community support, yet inability to get legislation passed, unlike in The Netherlands, Belgium and Oregon (inspired by the Dutch). This shows both the continuing polarisation in the community and the power of opposing lobby groups (particularly the medical and faith-based).

In Helga Kuhse's chapter, 'Accepting Responsibility: Dying in Australia and the Netherlands', in *Willing to Listen, Wanting to Die*,[14] she too argues that the open, honest Dutch approach is preferable to the Australian, and that Dutch society as a whole has accepted responsibility for 'the implementation of a procedural framework that will protect patients and doctors alike'.

Kuhse argues that for purposes of public policy, the two decisions of refusal of treatment and direct ending of life ought to be the same: the patient decides on a course of action that will lead to a dignified death, in consultation with the doctor, and the doctor carries it out. The key question here is whether it is contrary to the doctor's role to give such advice or to prescribe or administer drugs. The current polarisation on this point seems insurmountable in Australia.[15]

From the standpoint of this book, given that harm to others is the only argument that justifies restrictions in a liberal society, the distinction between 'direct' and 'indirect' ways of aiding a patient's dying should have no place in the framework of a liberal society.

It is a truism that because something is unlawful, this does not mean it is morally wrong. How else would moral progress be made? Examples abound – slavery, apartheid, racial and sexual discrimination. A law may merit censure and resistance and every effort to overturn it. There is also the deeper liberal argument that some areas of conduct are not properly the province of the law at all. In the case of euthanasia, as we have seen in this chapter and elsewhere, while the law may not permit, it may certainly hinder – by lack of clarity as well as specific sanctions.

The key questions, then, are:

- Is it sometimes legitimate for a person to choose death?
- If so, is this morally legitimate?
- If so, should it also be legally legitimate?
- If so, is it proper for doctors to be involved?

The argument and cases reviewed in this book point to the conclusion that all four should be answered in the affirmative.

Kuhse and Singer were longstanding colleagues at Monash University's Centre for Human Bioethics, and major figures in the euthanasia debate in Australia. They were involved in the study referred to in the previous chapter, where Australian doctors were surveyed by questionnaires modelled on the Remmelink survey in the Netherlands.[16] Their findings were that 1.8 per cent of all Australian deaths involving end-of-life decisions involved voluntary euthanasia or assisted suicide, and 3.5 per cent involved doctors ending life without the patient's explicit request.

Furthermore, 28.5 per cent involved withholding or withdrawing potentially life-prolonging treatment, and 30.9 per cent involved pain relief in large enough doses that life would probably be shortened. In thirty per cent of cases, medical decisions with the explicit intention of ending a patient's life were made – only four per cent in response to a patient's request. This led the survey to conclude that Australia had a higher rate of intentional ending of life without the patient's consent than The Netherlands – a troubling finding.

Helga Kuhse like Dr Syme, was president of the Voluntary Euthanasia Society of Victoria. The direct impact of her involvement in the issue is shown by the fact that a paper she wrote for a 1994 conference on Death, Dying and the Law, in Canberra, influenced Marshall Perron, then Chief Minister of the Northern Territory, to introduce enabling legislation.[17]

The Northern Territory experiment

As indicated at the start of this chapter, the Northern Territory's legislation – the Rights of the Terminally Ill Act – was overturned after only nine months by the federal Euthanasia Laws Act, introduced by Kevin Andrews as a Private Member's Bill. The Northern Territory Act, introduced as a Private Member's Bill by Marshall Perron, had been preceded by a review of the Natural Death Act 1989. At that time, Northern Territory legislation did not protect a patient's right to refuse unwanted medical treatment, nor protect doctors by permitting a defence of 'double effect' if they gave pain relief that hastened death. On the eve of the vote, Perron resigned as Chief Minister, and promised to resign from Parliament shortly afterwards, which he did – a politician of conviction.

The legislation was not implemented till 1 July 1997. There was a very short window of operation, with only four cases, two of them local. A High Court challenge was mounted by Chris Wake, President of the Northern Territory branch of the Australian Medical Association, who founded the Coalition Against Euthanasia, and Rev. Gondarra, an aboriginal Uniting Church minister. Wake also wrote to the then Prime Minister Keating, who refused to intervene, defending the Territory's jurisdiction, pronouncing it a valid law of the Northern Territory and saying that it was up to the people of the Northern Territory to express their views on the legislation rather than the Commonwealth.

The first person who came forward was a sixty-eight-year-old American woman with bowel cancer, who was a member of the Hemlock Society. She died naturally, as did Max Bell, another applicant who had come from Queensland after the legislation was passed, but before it was enacted, and left in disappointment. He was interviewed on the television programme 'Four Corners', which galvanised public opinion. After the Bell documentary, a Darwin surgeon who had refused to see Bell rang Nitschke, who had developed a suicide machine that provided a mechanical means of delivering the lethal dose, allowing the patient, not the doctor, to be the agent and other doctors were beginning to come forward by the time a third applicant, Bob Dent, came forward, in 1997. He was the first person to die under the Northern Territory Act.

It had originally been intended to have a residence requirement in the Northern Territory legislation, but Commonwealth provisions allowing free trade between states precluded that. Still, that would seem a desirable reform – even if only a short-term residency was required.[18]

The Act stated that a terminally ill patient, experiencing pain, suffering and distress to an extent deemed unacceptable, could request a medical practitioner for assistance to end his or her life. The doctor had to be satisfied on reasonable grounds that the illness was terminal and would result in the patient's death in the normal course and without application of extraordinary measures. A further requirement was that there were no medical measures acceptable to the patient which could reasonably be taken to effect a cure, and that any further treatment was only palliative in nature. The doctor needed to certify that the patient was of sound mind and making the decision freely, voluntarily and after due consideration.

A second medical practitioner, a resident of the Northern Territory, was required to examine the patient to confirm the presence and terminal nature of the illness, and to give an opinion on prognosis, to be recorded on the schedule used for certifications under the Act. The regulations required that this practitioner hold a qualification in a medical speciality related to the terminal illness, recognised by fellowship of a specialist college in Australia. If the first medical practitioner did not have special qualifications in palliative care, defined by the regulations as either two years' full-time practice in palliative medicine or not less than five years' general practice, a third doctor with such qualifications was required to give information to the patient on the availability of palliative care. A psychiatrist was also required to examine the patient and confirm that he or she was not suffering from a treatable clinical depression in respect of the illness.

The Act required a period of seven days to pass between the initial request to end life made to the first doctor and the patient's signing of an informed consent form, witnessed by two medical practitioners. A further forty-eight hours later, assistance to end life would be provided. A death as a result of assistance given under the Act was not taken to be unnatural, but a copy of the death certificate and relevant section of the medical record relating to the illness and death in each case had to be forwarded to the coroner. The coroner was subsequently required to report to Parliament the number of patients using the Act. So the procedures were comprehensive and rigorous.

As previously noted, Bob Dent was the first person to die under the Northern Territory legislation and sought Nitschke's help as soon as the legislation was enacted. He had been diagnosed with metastatic prostate cancer in 1991. Dent died on 22 September 1997, with Nitschke and his wife present, going to sleep in his wife's arms.

The day before he died, Dent wrote a moving letter to all federal parliamentarians, detailing his suffering, his gratitude that he had had the opportunity to use the Rights of the Terminally Ill Act, and his horror at 'newspaper stories of Kevin Andrews' attempts to overturn the most compassionate piece of legislation in the world'. He issued a powerful challenge:

> If you disagree with voluntary euthanasia, then don't use it, but don't deny me the right to use it if and when I want to … The Church and State must remain separate. What right has anyone because of their own religious faith (to which I don't subscribe) to demand that I behave according to their rules until some omniscient doctor decides that I must have had enough and increases my morphine until I die?[19]

Despite this plea, the Euthanasia Laws Act soon overturned the Northern Territory legislation.

It is worth stressing that none of the four people who died under the Northern Territory legislation[20] had been Nitschke's patients before, which compares adversely with the Dutch requirement that there be a longstanding relationship between doctor and patient, so that the doctor knew the patient's 'value history'.

Nitschke had became involved after hearing Chris Wake, president of the Northern Territory branch of the Australian Medical Association, claim that no doctor would provide euthanasia under the proposed legislation. Like Dr Kevorkian, his development of a suicide machine has led to him becoming involved with several Australian cases. Also like Dr Kevorkian, who had invented a similar machine his association may be said to be almost a liability to the cause – reflected in the description of him by Frank Devine as 'a kind of Scarlet Pimpernel'.[21]

When the Keating Labor government was defeated in 1996, Kevin Andrews found that the Wake-Gondarra High Court challenge named the federal government as well as the Northern Territory government as defendants. The federal government was seen as a party because it had not overturned the legislation. Andrews introduced a Private Member's Bill which was introduced into the House of Representatives in October, a month after Dent's death, and passed in December by 88 to 35. It passed through the Senate in March 1997 by 38 to 33 – a much narrower margin.[22]

The Northern Territory legislation is still on the books, and could be reactivated if the Northern Territory gains full statehood. However, in that event, so too would be the High Court challenge to the state's right to pass such legislation.

A valuable perspective on the Northern Territory experience is provided by a study conducted into 'Perspectives of Northern Territory Doctors, Nurses and Community Members on End-of-Life Decision-Making', by a University of Queensland team from the Department of Social and Preventive Medicine, in conjunction with the Centre for Social Research from Northern Territory University.[23] The study is particularly valuable because after completion of its survey, the intervention from the federal government to overturn the Northern Territory law made it the only one of its kind. The University of Queensland team is also responsible for an excellent series of research reports on the attitudes to euthanasia of community and allied and health professionals,[24] perspectives of general practitioners and patients,[25] directors of nursing of nursing homes, and of community and health professionals on end-of-life decision-making.[26]

In relation to the Northern Territory report, it identified a lack of knowledge of legal issues relating to end-of-life decision-making, with many health professionals and community members believing that suicide was a criminal offence – it is not, in any state or territory of Australia. Despite the Northern Territory Natural Death Act 1988 allowing a person to write a legally binding advance directive, or living will, few knew about such documents, and only 13 per cent of health professionals knew they were legally enforceable in the Northern Territory – a worrying figure, as is the finding that 10 per cent of health professionals believed that current enduring power of attorney legislation authorised the appointee to make medical decisions for another person rather than only financial and property matters. Importantly, 75 per cent of community members approved of the provisions of the Rights of the Terminally Ill Act.[27]

It is significant that the factors of greatest concern to community members regarding future terminal illness were:

• loss of mental faculties – seventy-seven per cent;
• loss of control – seventy-six per cent;
• loss of independence – sixty-seven per cent;
• fear of being a burden to family – sixty-one per cent;
• loss of dignity – sixty per cent;
• leaving loved ones – fifty-seven per cent;
• fear of protracted dying – fifty-one per cent;
• physical pain – forty-eight per cent.

Death itself was of lesser concern – eighteen per cent. However, health professionals ranked physical pain as of greatest concern to their patients.

Interestingly, community members were more in favour than health professionals of a doctor being allowed by law to assist a terminally ill patient to die (seventy-three per cent to fifty-nine per cent) and of a doctor complying with a patient's request to turn off a life-support system (seventy-one per cent to fifty-eight per cent). The report highlighted the lack of consistent legislation on end-of-life issues, with variations from state to state; only South Australia, Victoria, the Australian Capital Territory and the Northern Territory then had any living will legislation in place (Queensland passed the Powers of Attorney Act in 1998). Importantly, a solid majority of both groups (eighty-three per cent community members, and seventy-one per cent health professionals) did not believe that a policy of active voluntary euthanasia would undermine the basic trust between patients and care-givers.

While there will always be difficult judgements to be made in this contested area of choice and death, a workable legal framework would be a good (and necessary) starting point.

The Nancy Crick case 2002

The Nancy Crick case of 2002 shows yet again the glaring effects of the absence of such a clear and effective legal framework.

Nancy Crick, sixty-nine years old, suffering from bowel cancer, who had undergone three operations and had a colostomy bag, was constantly ill. Offered further surgery, she refused. She wanted to end her life, but also wanted to die surrounded by family and friends. She contacted Dr Nitschke, and became a campaigner for voluntary euthanasia, holding a press conference in February 2002, announcing that she was going to kill herself if no one could, or would, do it for her. She wanted to avoid being fed and changed, and to act while she still could. She attracted widespread media interest around the country – over print, radio, television and the internet. She kept a web journal and obtained her lethal medication over the internet.

She was persuaded to seek palliative care, but it was only partially successful and she checked herself out.

Though suicide is not a criminal offence in Queensland, aiding, abetting and assisting suicide is. She invited twenty-one people to be present (Dr Nitschke was not one of them) and had multiple keys cut to her house to minimise the risk of prosecution of any of those present. Certainly, this may be seen as a clever device to fragment the responsibility and circumvent the law. It may also be seen as convivial. She had a party that was also a wake, with sandwiches for her guests, took barbiturates, had a cigarette and a sip of Bailey's liqueur, and died twenty minutes later. The authorities were notified the next morning. Dr Nitschke's medical records in Adelaide and Darwin were searched by police.[28] Not until 8 March 2004 was he cleared.

Nancy Crick's home was declared a 'crime scene' and her body was not released for burial for several days, while an autopsy was conducted. Those present were in limbo as to whether they would be charged. Only one friend, the Tasmanian director of Exit, 'outed' himself as being present. Those who were there 'assisted' in the original sense of being present, not of rendering aid. Such a death – prepared and among family and friends – may be seen as infinitely preferable to some of the furtive, lonely, guilt-ridden deaths described earlier in this chapter.

When the autopsy results found she did not have cancer, but an inoperable twisted bowel, there was criticism that she was not suffering a terminal illness, as if this somehow invalidated her action. Those in favour of euthanasia insisted that continuing and unbearable suffering was sufficient motivation for a rational suicide. Certainly Nancy Crick exited with flair. She could have acted privately, but clearly wanted her death to make a difference in galvanising the campaign for voluntary euthanasia – as it did. She wanted to inform and engage the public and did that, though with limited success. The Queensland Premier's immediate response was that it would not prompt change to the Queensland law – and indeed, it has not.

What has lead to more criticism is that it was not until 18 June 2004 that the twenty-one were informed that a prosecution would not ensue. There seemed no time limit. No one in authority was willing to draw a line under the case, so it seemed to have lapsed rather than reached closure. In terms of the old adage 'justice delayed is justice denied', this must be the maximally unsatisfactory outcome.

At the Australian Medical Association conference which took place the following weekend, a few days after Nancy Crick's death, Dr Nitschke moved a motion to adopt a neutral position on euthanasia. It was defeated, but by a narrower margin than before. The 'double effect' doctrine was convincingly endorsed, supporting doctors whose 'primary intent is to relieve the suffering and distress of terminally ill patients in accordance with patients' wishes and interests, even though a foreseen secondary consequence is the hastening of death'. This principle, and the practice of terminal sedation which it endorses, in effect allow de facto euthanasia, though, as we have seen, Dr Syme regarded the difference between euthanasia and terminal sedation as hair-splitting and hypocritical.

One final case under another jurisdiction, in South Australia, deserves mention. Shirley Nolan, who had been suffering from Parkinson's disease for twenty-five years, took her own life. She too was not terminally ill, but attracted great public sympathy as she had established the world's first bone marrow donor registry in 1971, after her son Anthony was born with Wiscott-Aldrich syndrome and died when he was only eight. The paradox of the woman who had been giving the 'gift of life' for thirty years becoming 'an advocate for death' for herself was poignant.

There the issue rests in Australia. But the risk is that differing state laws are played off against one another, or against Commonwealth legislation. Activists in Australia now seem to be trying to work via legislation, rather than the courts.

It is surely unacceptable in a civilised society that anyone could be driven to an end that is as sickening, tragic and fraught with risk as that of an eighty-five-year-old Perth man, who manoeuvred his wheelchair off a Perth jetty because he was suffering unbearably from throat cancer and could not find a doctor to help him die. Is it really beyond the scope of reason and goodwill to learn from experience in other countries and adopt good practices, in advance of the excruciating cases that only reinvent an inexorable wheel?

There remain many hard questions. If euthanasia were legal, would an individual then have the right to request it in an advance directive? And what effect would legalising it have on society?

From a utilitarian perspective, a necessary argument would be that change would benefit society as a whole. Utilitarianism from its inception under Jeremy Bentham and then J. S. Mill was a free-thinking, perfectibilist philosophy, wedded to social reform and practical policy, and believing in the possibility of enlightenment and progress. It remains so today – whether the Millian utilitarianism advocated in this book or the preference utilitarianism of the best known contemporary utilitarian, Peter Singer – which is why utilitarian arguments must be persuasive from the perspective of the good of society as well as the good of the individual.

Notes

1. J. Morgan, ed., *An Easeful Death* (Sydney: Federation Press, 1996), p. 206.
2. H. Kuhse, *Willing to Listen, Wanting to Die* (Harmondsworth: Penguin, 1994), p. 172.
3. Ibid., p. 174.
4. Ibid., p. 184.
5. Gardner; *re BWV*, VSC 173, 29 May 2003.
6. Morgan, ed., *An Easeful Death*, p. 194.
7. Gardner; *re BWV*.
8. Kuhse, *Willing to Listen, Wanting to Die*, p. 84.
9. Ibid., p. 9.
10. M. Cosic, *The Right to Die?* (Melbourne: New Holland Publishers, 2003), p. 177.
11. Kuhse, *Willing to Listen, Wanting to Die*, p. 155.
12. Ibid., p. 171.
13. Cosic, *The Right to Die?*, p. 191.
14. Kuhse, *Willing to Listen, Wanting to Die*, p. 246.
15. R. Ho, 'Assessing Attitudes Towards Euthanasia: An Analysis of the Subcategorical Approach to Right to Die Issues', *Personality and Individual Differences* Vol. 25 (1998).
16. Kuhse, *Willing to Listen, Wanting to Die*; H. Kuhse and P. Singer, 'Euthanasia: A Survey of Nurses' Attitudes and Practices', *The Australian Nurses Journal* Vol. 21 (1992); H. Kuhse et al., 'End-of-Life Decisions in Australian Medical Practice', *Medical Journal of Australia* 157 (1997).
17. Cosic, *The Right to Die?*, p. 167.
18. D. W. Kissane, A. Street and P. Nitschke, '7 Deaths in Darwin: Case Studies under the Rights of the Terminally Ill Act Northern Territory Australia', *The Lancet* Vol. 352 (1998).
19. I. Sharon and James W., Walters Fraser, 'Death – Whose Decision? Physician-Assisted Dying and the Terminally Ill', *Western Journal of Medicine* Vol. 176, No. 2 (2002).
20. D. Kissane, 'Case Presentation: A Case of Euthanasia, the Northern Territory, Australia', *Journal of Pain and Symptom Management* Vol. 19, No. 6 (2000).
21. F. Devine, 'An Interview with Philip Nitschke', *Quadrant* Vol. 46, No. 10 (2002).
22. S. Broughton and S. Palmieri, 'Gendered Contributions to Parliamentary Debates: The Case of Euthanasia', *Australian Journal of Political Science* Vol. 34, No. 1 (1999).
23. C. M. Cartwright et al., *End-of-Life Decision-Making: Perspectives of*

Northern Territory Doctors, Nurses and Community Members (University of Queensland, 1998).

24. M. A. Steinberg et al., *Perspectives of Directors of Nursing of Nursing Homes on End-of-Life Decision-Making* (University of Queensland, 1996).

25. M. A. Steinberg et al., *Healthy Ageing, Healthy Dying: Community and Health Professional Perspective on End-of-Life Decision-Making* (University of Queensland, 1996).

26. M. A. Steinberg et al., *End-of-Life Decision-Making: Perspectives of General Practitioners and Patients* (University of Queensland, 1996).

27. Morgan, ed., *An Easeful Death*.

28. C. Zinn, 'Police Seize Computer Files of Euthanasia Campaigner in Cancer Case', *British Medical Journal* Vol. 3757, No. 7360 (2002).

Conclusion

Few issues are more controversial and divide public opinion more passionately than that of euthanasia. This is hardly surprising, as it goes to the heart of our deepest beliefs about human nature and the moral value of human life. Any assault on these beliefs can take on the character not of a tolerable difference of individual taste but of a religious war. This might be expected in a fundamentalist, authoritarian, theocratic society, where a state religion holds sway and dissent is not to be brooked, but it is a deeply disturbing threat in a liberal democracy, fundamentally grounded on a separation between church and state, and a commitment to individual liberty and toleration of differences, within the rule of law.

The scope of this book applies to liberal democratic societies. All four countries examined – America, England, The Netherlands, Australia – are liberal democracies. It is unavoidable that liberal democratic societies grapple with the problem of how to deal with the extending human life span that medical advances have delivered us, and the related problem of how to use the spectacular and continuing scientific and medical developments for good. Both utopian and dystopian views are held. The current controversy over euthanasia may on the one hand be seen as partly the product of our medical success, and on the other as another example of the ongoing struggle to see that the technological tail does not wag the human dog.

It has been argued here that the notion of choice is central to the notion of the human person and the dignity of the human being. As the Existentialist philosopher Jean-Paul Sartre argued in so many of his writings, acts of choice are constitutive of the individual. On this view, mankind first of all exists and then defines himself by his actions. He cannot appeal to external values or rules or an innate human nature or essence to rationalise what he does or displace his responsibility for his actions. A life is a tapestry woven out of acts of choice. There is no option but self-realisation, and the focus is on particular situations. We improvise our way through life, conferring value by the acts we choose. For Sartre man is 'the choosing being'. It is consistent with such a standpoint that such a being would also exercise choice in relation to their own death – and extend it to others.

Mill's liberal utilitarian account also places choice at the hub of what it is to be a human being, though for Mill, unlike Sartre, there is an objective rational basis for moral decisions, and there is value, purpose and meaning in the world. For Mill, the source of value is utility, or the greatest happiness principle. On this view, actions are right in proportion as they produce happiness and wrong as they produce unhappiness. Happiness means pleasure and absence of pain; unhappiness, pain and absence of pleasure.

Happiness on Mill's account, however, amounted to self-realisation, and Mill's ethical utilitarianism was reinforced by his political philosophy of liberalism in arguing for the maximum sphere of liberty for the individual within society.

Mill famously deplored paternalistic interference and argued that society is entitled to interfere only with the liberty of action of an individual to prevent harm to others – not for his own good, either physical or moral.

This anti-paternalist perspective continues to resonate in the euthanasia debate, as the arguments are applied, tacitly or explicitly, to problematic issues involving the proper calibration of the domains of individual liberty and the state, and how this is best done in a way that is both liberal and democratic.

The other pole of the choice and death axis – death – forces us to move on from a simple account of biological death to consideration of the notion at the root of the euthanasia debate of what is meant by a 'good death'.

The inexorable progress from the development of the ventilator to pressures concerning organ donation have challenged our understanding of how to deal with a whole range of difficult medical cases, from severely disabled newborns to the comatose or suffering adult. It is clear that pronouncing death is not a simple recognition of a brute biological fact, but a contestable sphere of judgement and further medical action. The apparently simple question 'When does a human being die?' (or its variants 'When is a human being dead?', 'When has a human being died?') dissolves into arbitrariness and ambiguity, while what is at stake on the issue ranges from the possibility of organ donation to the simple recognition that further treatment is futile, that consciousness no longer exists in the patient and that sometimes it is in the best interest of a patient to be let die.

I have described here some of the conceptual struggles this dilemma has posed, as people sought to negotiate stark choices with the aid of distinctions such as ordinary or extraordinary means of treatment; killing or letting die; acts or omissions; foreseen but unintended effects. I have argued that these distinctions can be useful as a way of justifying and guiding practice, where one alternative of the binary oppositions is seen as acceptable. But in the case of ordinary or extraordinary, killing and letting die, and acts and omissions, the boundaries have been challenged, so that the defensive potential blurs. 'Foreseen but unintended effect', however, remains intact, and influential – even if contested.

These distinctions are implicit in the notion of euthanasia itself, which became bifurcated into voluntary or involuntary and active or passive euthanasia.

Four possible types of euthanasia are thus generated. In voluntary active euthanasia, the doctor deliberately acts to cause death, such as by injecting a lethal dose of drugs, at the patient's request. In voluntary passive euthanasia, the doctor suspends treatment, at the patient's request, thereby hastening the patient's death. In-voluntary active euthanasia, death is caused by actions taken without reference to the patient's wishes, and in involuntary passive euthanasia, death is caused by omission or withholding of treatment, carried out without reference to the patient's wishes. In both the involuntary cases, the argument may be put that the action was taken in the patient's interest or to reduce the patient's suffering.

Voluntary active euthanasia may be seen as the most readily defensible, then voluntary passive euthanasia, followed by involuntary passive euthanasia and involuntary active euthanasia. It is slippery slope arguments of inevitable progression – or descent – from voluntary active to involuntary active euthanasia that remain the strongest secular arguments against euthanasia, after the religiously-based sanctity of life argument – the argument that human life is sacred and should never be taken. The strongest and most common argument put in favour of voluntary euthanasia rests on individual autonomy and the right to choose, followed by arguments based on preservation of human dignity and alleviation of suffering.

The debate currently centres on voluntary euthanasia and assisted suicide, which are the strongest cases for euthanasia, involving as they do conscious patients who need medical assistance to die – or be 'let die'.

A key purpose in reviewing these conceptual distinctions is to find a way of making the doctor's role acceptable, by avoiding classifying euthanasia as either deliberate killing or – even more reprehensible – murder, or wrongful killing.

The double effect doctrine of 'foreseen but unintended effect' remains the mandatory defence for a doctor who hastens or assists a patient's death in all jurisdictions but The Netherlands. The issue of euthanasia is thus both a moral and a legal problem.

The basic moral question is whether euthanasia is ever permissible in any circumstances. A further boundary question is raised of whether it should be seen as outside the domain of the law. It is a liberal axiom that the spheres of morality and law are distinct, and that the law should not be used to enforce a morality. Going back to Mill, this is the argument that self-regarding actions, or actions that affect others only with their free, undeceived consent, are not the domain of the state at all. Distaste or disapproval may be the only appropriate responses, rather than sanctions or punishment. Given the harm principle as the only basis for action against an individual, and the strictures against paternalistic interference, on this view a case needs to be made that the issue falls within the ambit of the law. Similar arguments have been made on issues such as prostitution, pornography and censorship, homosexuality and compulsory seatbelts.

The basic legal question is whether euthanasia should be punished or, at the other extreme, legalised. If it is to be regulated by the law, should this be by legislation and the criminal courts, or could it be devolved (as well or instead) to a statutory body responsible for medical regulation? If it is to be legalised – or decriminalised – what effect would this have on society, and would an individual then have the right to request medical assistance in an advance directive – subject to the willingness of the doctor involved?

These are the issues that have been discussed here, along with the problems of achieving consensus, even concerning resource allocation choices. The Oregon scheme and the QALY approach were examined as two attempted decision procedures, but as the choices involved are not purely economic, both lead back to the central question of the relative role of the individual and the state. In the context of Mill's liberalism, on the question of euthanasia the only reliable judge of quality of life is the agent involved.

Against this theoretical groundwork, Part Two focused on the approach taken to euthanasia in four selected countries: America, England, The Netherlands and Australia. Each of these countries represents different political systems and differing approaches to regulation, and in each of them the debate has evolved in a different way, although the cases which have arisen, many of which are discussed here, display many similarities. The differences lie in matters of emphasis, and how the issue was managed – or merely accommodated.

Many of the most significant developments have occurred only in the very recent past. In America the Schiavo case precipitated state intervention in the context of conservative initiatives in relation to privacy, medical records and partial birth abortions. In England, the Diane Pretty case of 2002 seemed a setback to the apparent recognition of quality of life issues signalled by the House of Lords decision in the Tony Bland case of 1993. New legislation is pending as a result of a Private Member's Bill in the House of Lords, which may reverse the 1994 legislation and allow assisted suicide for terminally ill patients. In The Netherlands, 39 years of de facto recognition of voluntary euthanasia and assisted suicide under strict medical guidelines was translated into legislation in April 2002. In Australia an uneasy truce prevails, despite the highly publicised voluntary euthanasia of Nancy Crick in 2002, after the federal government moved swiftly to overturn the Northern Territory legislation permitting voluntary euthanasia and assisted suicide in 1997.

In considering the experiences of these four countries, I believe that some conclusions can be drawn which are, on the whole, positive and which justify cautious optimism that progress can be made. They have in fact created a body of experience that can be drawn on allowing for differences between countries, such as the special conditions that prevail in The Netherlands which help make it progressive. The precedents they set make the issue not so difficult, less intractable. Dworkin's triple classification of patients into conscious and competent, unconscious and incompetent, and conscious and incompetent helps avoid an 'all-or-nothing' approach. Reasoned distinctions can be made, which ground differences in practices that can be regulated and managed, without leading pell-mell down the slippery slope feared by opponents of voluntary euthanasia.

Good examples of possible guidelines in terms of eligibility for voluntary euthanasia are provided by both Oregon and Rotterdam. The Oregon Death with Dignity Act stipulated that a patient has to be aged eighteen or over, a resident of the state, capable of making and communicating a clear decision, and terminally ill, with a prognosis of under six months to live. The Rotterdam criteria were along similar lines: the patient had to have made a voluntary request, the request must be well considered, the wish for death must be enduring, and the patient had to be suffering unbearably. Similar conditions were written into the short-lived Northern Territory legislation in Australia.

In terms of procedure, the Bay Area of California guidelines stipulated that a private health care physician who received a request for assisted suicide must make an initial referral to a hospice programme or to a physician experienced in palliative care. The Coalition of Hospice professionals noted that regulation of physician-assisted suicide would mandate that all palliative measures be exhausted as a condition precedent to assisted suicide.

These are common-sense safeguards to ensure that any requests for euthanasia are not driven by pain that could be better managed. Some such regulations would surely be adopted by any country considering introducing legalised voluntary euthanasia and assisted suicide, and this may provide an answer to many of the doubts expressed about the proposal.

One clear conclusion is that it is better to have legislation that even only partly permits voluntary euthanasia if this reflects the consensus in a particular society and is owned by that society, rather than have legislation forbidding it, which is not clear or not applied. Furthermore, legislation is not the only way to regulate. Expert committees and medical regulation also have a role to play, and the structure, balance and emphasis would vary according to the ethos of different countries. That level of detail and specificity can best be left to each individual country.

The key arguments – the wheels that turn – are the ones that have been put throughout, concerning the centrality of choice to the individual and the necessity for the state to respect individual autonomy in the area of choice and death – and to tread as lightly as necessary regulation and legal safeguards allow. An ethical consensus concerning euthanasia can then emerge, befitting the aspirations of a liberal democratic society.

It is hoped that the arguments put forward in this book have contributed to the reader's understanding, as both an individual and a citizen of a society, and so in some way assisted personal reflection, social debate and wise policy on the sensitive and contentious issue of euthanasia.

References

Amarasekara, Kumar. 'Autonomy, Paternalism and Discrimination: The Darker Side of Euthanasia'. In *Legal Visions of the 21st Century*, edited by A. Angie and G. Sturgess. The Hague: Kluwer Law International, 1998.

Asch, D. A., J. A. Shea, M. K. Jedeziewski and C. L. Bosk. 'The Limits of Suffering: Critical Care Nurses' Views of Hospital Care at the End of Life'. *Social Science Medicine* Vol. 45, No. 11 (1997).

Ashcroft, Richard. 'Euthanasia, Regulation and Slippery Slopes'. *Palliative Medicine* Vol. 17 (2003).

Banninck, M., A. R. Van Gool, A. van der Heide and P. J. van der Haas. 'Psychiatric Consultation and Quality of Decision Making in Euthanasia'. *The Lancet* Vol. 356, No. 16 (December 2000).

Birchard, Karen. 'Serial Killer Doctor Sparks Calls for Legislation Changes'. *Medical Post* Vol. 39, No. 29 (2003).

Bostrom, Barry A. 'Knight v. Beverly Health Care Centre: In the Supreme Court of Alabama'. *Issues in Law and Medicine* Vol. 17, No. 2 (2001).

Broughton, S. and S. Palmieri. 'Gendered Contributions to Parliamentary Debates: The Case of Euthanasia'. *Australian Journal of Political Science* Vol. 34, No. 1 (1999): 29.

Campbell, N. 'A Problem for the Idea of Voluntary Euthanasia'. *Journal of Medical Ethics* Vol. 25, No. 3 (1999).

Campbell, R. 'Life, Death and the Law'. In *Introducing Applied Ethics*, edited by Brenda Almond. Oxford: Blackwell, 1995.

Cartwright, C. M., G. W. Robinson, M. A. Steinberg, G. Williams, J. N. Nathan and W. B. Tyler. *End-of-Life Decision-Making: Perspectives of Northern Territory Doctors, Nurses and Community Members*. University of Queensland, 1998.

Caton, H. 'The Resource Allocation Dilemma'. *Health Cover* Vol. 2, No. 4 (1993).

Charlesworth, M. *Bioethics in a Liberal Society*. Cambridge: Cambridge University Press, 1993.

143

Clark Jr, R. T. 'Baby Jose'. *JAMA* Vol. 284, No. 9 (2000).

Cohen-Almagor, R. 'Culture of Death in the Netherlands: Dutch Perspectives'. *Issues in Law and Medicine* Vol. 17, No. 2 (2001).

—'Why the Netherlands?' *Journal of Law, Medicine and Ethics* Vol. 30, No. 1 (2002).

Cosic, M. *The Right to Die?* Melbourne: New Holland Publishers, 2003.

Culver, C. M. and B. Gert. 'The Definition and Criterion of Death'. In *Biomedical Ethics*, edited by T. A. Mappes and J. Zembaty. New York: McGraw-Hill, 1991.

Cuttini, M., M. Nadai, M. Kaminski, G. Hansen, R. de Leeuw, S. Lenoir, J. Persson, M. Rebagliato, M. Reid, U. de Vonderweid, H. G. Lenard, M. Orzalesi and R. Saracci. 'End-of-Life Decisions in Neonatal Intensive Care: Physician's Self-Reported Practices in 7 European Countries'. *The Lancet* Vol. 355, No. 17 (June 2000).

Deliens, L. and G. van der Waal. 'The Euthanasia Laws in Belgium and the Netherlands'. *The Lancet* Vol. 362 (2003).

Deliens, L., F. Mortier, J. Bilsen, M. Cosyns, R. Vander Stichele, J. Vanoverloop and K. Ingels. 'End-of-Life Decisions in Medical Practice in Flanders, Belgium: A Nationwide Survey'. *The Lancet* Vol. 356, No. 25 (November 2000).

Derse, A. R. 'Is There a Lingua Franca for Bioethics at the End of Life?' *Journal of Law, Medicine and Ethics* Vol. 28, No. 3 (2000).

Devine, F. 'An Interview with Philip Nitschke'. *Quadrant* Vol. 46, No. 10 (2002): 44.

Devlin, P. *The Enforcement of Morals*. Oxford: Oxford University Press, 1968.

Diamond, B. 'Should Diane Pretty's Husband Be Allowed to Help Her to Die?' *British Journal of Nursing* Vol. 11, No. 9 (2002).

Doyal, L. and L. Doyal. 'Why Active Euthanasia and Physician-Assisted Suicide Should Be Legalised'. *British Medical Journal* Vol. 323, No. 10 (November 2001).

Dworkin, R. *Life's Dominion*. London: HarperCollins, 1998.

Dyer, C. 'Public Inquiry Hears How Shipman Killed Patients with Diamorphine'. *BMJ* Vol. 323 (2001).

Dyer, O. 'Shipman Murdered More Than 200 Patients, Inquiry Ends'. *British Medical Journal* Vol. 325, No. 7357 (2000).

English, V., J. Gardner, G. Romano-Critchley and A. Summerville. 'Legislation on Euthanasia'. *Journal of Medical Ethics* Vol. 27 (2001).

Erikson, E. H. *Childhood and Society*. New York: W. W. Norton, 1950.

— *Identity, Youth and Crisis*. New York: W. W. Norton, 1968.

Finlay, N. G., and B. van Dijk. 'Euthanasia: The Dutch Experience and What It Entails in Practice'. *The Lancet Oncology* Vol. 3 (March 2002).

Fitzpatrick, M. 'Auditing Deaths'. *The Lancet* Vol. 362 (2003).

Fletcher, J. *Situation Ethics*. London: SCM, 1966.

Frader, J. E. 'Baby Doe Blinders.' *JAMA* Vol. 284, No. 6 (September 2000).

Fraser, Sharon I. and Walters, James W. 'Death – Whose Decision? Physician-Assisted Dying and the Terminally Ill'. *Western Journal of Medicine* 176, No. 2 (2002): 120.

Gilligan, C. *In a Different Voice*. Cambridge, MA: Harvard University Press, 1982.

Glick, H. R. and A. Hutchinson. 'The Rising Agenda of Physician-Assisted Suicide'. *Policy Studies Journal* Vol. 27 (2004).

Goodnough, Abby. 'Governor of Florida Orders Woman Fed in Right-to-Die Case'. *New York Times*, 22 October 2003.

Gorsuch, N. M. 'The Right to Assisted Suicide and Euthanasia'. *Harvard Journal of Law and Public Policy* Vol. 23, No. 3 (2000).

Gross, M. L. 'Abortion and Neonaticide: Ethics, Practice and Policy in 4 Nations'. *Bioethics* Vol. 16, No. 3 (2002).

— 'Avoiding Anomalous Newborns: Pre-emptive Abortion Treatment Thresholds and the Case of Baby Messenger'. *Journal of Medical Ethics* 26, No. 4 (2000).

Harris, J. 'Consent and End of Life Decisions'. *Journal of Medical Ethics* Vol. 29, No. 1 (2003).

Hart, H. L. A. *Law, Liberty and Morality*. Oxford: Oxford University Press, 1968.

Haverkate, I., G. van der Wal, P. J. van der Maas, B. D. Onwuteaka-Philipsen and P. J. Kostense. 'Guidelines on Euthanasia and Pain Alleviation: Compliance and Opinions of Physicians'. *Health Policy* Vol. 44 (1998).

Hendin, H. 'The Dutch Experience'. *Issues in Law and Medicine* Vol. 17, No. 3 (2003).

Hershenov, D. 'The Problematic Role of Irreversibility in the Definition of Death'. *Bioethics* Vol. 17, No. 1 (2003).

Ho, R. 'Assessing Attitudes Towards Euthanasia: An Analysis of the Subcategorical Approach to Right to Die Issues'. *Personality and Individual Differences* Vol. 25 (1998).

Hoffmann, Bill. 'Coma Man Awakes from 19-Year Slumber'. *New York Post*, No. 10 (July 2003).

Hoge, W. 'Paralysed Woman Has Right to Die: A British Judge Rules'. *New York Times*, 23 March 2002.

Horsfall, S., C. Alcocer, C. Temple-Duncan and J. Polk. 'Views of Euthanasia from an East Texas University'. *Social Science Journal* Vol. 38 (2001).

Hull, R. T. 'The Case for Physician-Assisted Suicide'. *Free Inquiry* Vol. 23, No. 3 (2003).

Huxtable, R. and A. V. Campbell. 'Palliative Care and the Euthanasia Debate: Recent Developments'. *Palliative Medicine* Vol. 17 (2003): 94–5.

Jaggar, A. 'Feminist Ethics: Some Issues for the Nineties'. *Journal of Social Philosophy* 20, No. 1/2 (1989).

Johnstone, M. J. *Bioethics: A Nursing Perspective*. Sydney: W. B. Saunders/Baillière Tindall, 1989.

Kass, L. R. *Life, Liberty and the Defense of Dignity*. San Francisco: Encounter Books, 2002.

Kater, L., R. Houtepen, R. De Vries and G. Widdershoven. 'Health Care Ethics and Health Law in the Dutch Discussion on End-of-Life Decisions: A Historical Analysis of the Dynamics and Development of Both Disciplines'. *Studies in History and Philosophy of Biological and Biomedical Sciences* Vol. 34 (2003).

Kerridge, L. H. 'Death, Dying and Donation: Organ Transplantation and the Dignity of Death'. *Issues in Law and Medicine* Vol. 18, No. 1 (2002).

Kinnell, H. G. 'Serial Homicide by Doctors: Shipman in Perspective'. *BMJ* Vol. 321 (2000).

Kissane, D. 'Case Presentation: A Case of Euthanasia, the Northern Territory, Australia'. *Journal of Pain and Symptom Management* Vol. 19, No. 6 (2000).

Kissane, D. W., A. Street and P. Nitschke. '7 Deaths in Darwin: Case Studies under the Rights of the Terminally Ill Act Northern Territory Australia'. *The Lancet* Vol. 352 (1998).

Kohlberg, L. *The Philosophy of Moral Development: Moral Stages and the Idea of Justice*. San Francisco: Harper & Row, 1981.

Kübler-Ross, E. *On Death and Dying*. London: Routledge, 1989.

Kuhse, H. 'Accepting Responsibility: Dying in Australia and the Netherlands'. In *Willing to Listen, Wanting to Die*, edited by H. Kuhse. Harmondsworth: Penguin, 1994.

— 'Euthanasia'. In *A Companion to Ethics*, edited by P. Singer. Oxford: Blackwell, 1993, p. 294.

— *Willing to Listen, Wanting to Die*. Harmondsworth: Penguin, 1994.

Kuhse, H. and P. Singer. 'Euthanasia: A Survey of Nurses' Attitudes and Practices'. *The Australian Nurses Journal* Vol. 21 (1992): 71.

Kuhse, H., P. Singer, P. Baume, M. Clark, and M. Rickard. 'End-of-Life Decisions in Australian Medical Practice'. *Medical Journal of Australia* 157 (1997).

Kuhse, Helga. 'A Modern Myth. That Letting Die is not the Intentional Causation of Death: Some Reflections on the Trial and Acquittal of Dr Leonard Arthur'. *Journal of Applied Philosophy* Vol. 1, No. 1 (1984): 21–38.

Langley, A. '"Suicide Tourists" Go to the Swiss for Help in Dying'. *New York Times* (4 February 2003).

Liptak, Adam. 'Ruling Upholds Oregon Law Authorising Assisted Suicide'. *New York Times*, 27 May 2004.

Lund, N. 'Why Ashcroft is Wrong on Assisted Suicide'. *Commentary* Vol. 113, No. 2 (2002).

Maslow, A. *The Farther Reaches of Human Nature*. Harmondsworth: Penguin, 1971.

— *Toward a Psychology of Being*. New York: Van Nostrand, 1968.

Materstvedt, L. J. and S. Kaasa. 'Euthanasia and Physician-Assisted Suicide in Scandinavia'. *Palliative Medicine* (2002).

McConnell, T. 'On an Alleged Problem for Voluntary Euthanasia'. *Journal of Medical and Ethics* Vol. 26, No. 3 (2000).

McCullagh, P. 'Euthanasia and Attitudes towards Others: Why is it an Issue Now?' In *Euthanasia, Palliative and Hospice Care and the Terminally Ill*, edited by J. Stuparich. Canberra: Right to Life Association, 1992.

McHaffie, H. E. 'Withholding/Withdrawing Treatment from Neonates: Legislation and Official Guidelines across Europe'. *Journal of Medical Ethics* Vol. 25, No. 6 (1999).

McStay, R. 'Terminal Sedation: Palliative Care for Intractable Pain, Post Glucksberg and Quill'. *American Journal of Law and Medicine* Vol. 29, No. 1 (2003): 45.

Mill, J. S. *Collected Works*. Toronto: University of Toronto Press.

— *Three Essays*. Oxford: Oxford University Press, 1978.

Molloy, W. *Vital Choices*. Harmondsworth: Penguin, 1994.

Moreland, J. P. 'James Rachels and the Active Euthanasia Debate'. *JETS* 31/1 (1988).

Morgan, J., ed. *An Easeful Death*. Sydney: Federation Press, 1996.

Naik, G. 'Last Requests: The Grim Mission of a Swiss Group: Visitors' Suicides'. *Wall Street Journal*, 22 November 2002.

National Health and Medical Research Council (NHMRC). 'Certifying Death: The Brain Function Criterion'. 1997.

— 'Donating Organs after Death: Ethical Issues'. 1997.

Nicholson, R. 'Death Is the Remedy?' *Hastings Center Report* Vol. 32, No. 1 (2002).

Nussbaum, M. *Women and Human Development*. Cambridge: Cambridge University Press, 2000.

Nussbaum, M. and J. Glover. *Women, Culture and Development*. Oxford: Clarendon Press, 1995.

Onwuteaka-Philipsen, B. D., A. van der Heide, D. Koper, I. Keif-Deerenberg, J. A. C. Rietjens, M. L. Rerup, A. M. Vrakking, J. J. Georges, M. T. Muller, Gerrit van der Wal and P. J. van der Maas. 'Euthanasia and Other End-of-Life Decisions in the Netherlands in 1990, 1995 and 2001'. *The Lancet* Vol. 362 (2003).

Onwuteaka-Philipsen, L. and G. van der Wal. 'A Protocol for Consulting of Another Physician in Cases of Euthanasia and Assisted Suicide'. *Journal of Medical Ethics* Vol. 22, No. 8 (2001).

Paul, P. 'Euthanasia and Assisted Suicide'. *American Demographics*, Vol. 24, No. 10 (November 2002).

Persson, D. 'Human Death – a View from the Beginning of Life'. *Bioethics* Vol. 16, No. 1 (2002).

President's Commission for the Study of Ethical Problems in Medicine and Biomedical and Behavioural Research. 'Why "Update" Death?'. In

Biomedical Ethics, edited by T. Mappes and J. Zembaty. New York: McGraw-Hill, 1981, p. 388.

Quill, T. 'Death and Dignity: A Case of Individualised Decision'. *New England Journal of Medicine* Vol. 324 (1991): pp. 691–4.

Rawls, J., J. J. Thomson, R. Nagel, R. Dworkin, T. M. Scanlan and T. Nagel. 'Assisted Suicide: The Philosophers' Brief'. *The New York Review of Books*, 27 March 1997.

Richmond, C. 'Medical Murders Shock England'. *Canadian Medical Association Journal* Vol. 163, No. 5 (2000).

Rikkert, M. G. M. O. and W. H. L. Hoefnagels. 'Nutrition in the Terminal Stages of Life in Nursing-Home Patients'. *Age and Ageing* Vol. 30 (2001).

Rogers, E. H. 'A Federalism of Convenience'. *Human Rights* Vol. 29, No. 4 (Fall 2002).

Roscoe, L. A., J. E. Malphurs, L. J. Dragovic and D. Cohen. 'A Comparison of Characteristics of Kevorkian Euthanasia Cases and Physician-Assisted Suicides in Oregon'. *The Gerontologist* Vol. 41, No. 4 (2001).

Rowland, R. *Living Laboratories*. Sydney: Sun, 1992.

Sanderson, M. A. 'European Convention on Human Rights-Assisted Suicide: Pretty v. UK'. *American Journal of International Law* (2002).

Sartre, J-P. 'Existentialism is a Humanism'. In *Existentialism*, edited by W Kaufmann. New York: World Publishing Company, 1972.

Saunders, Dame Cicely. 'From the UK'. *Palliative Medicine* 17 (2003): 102–3.

Seale, C. 'Changing Patterns of Death and Dying'. *Social Science and Medicine* Vol. 51 (2000).

Shannon, T. A. 'Killing Them Softly with Kindness: Euthanasia Legislation in the Netherlands'. *America* Vol. 185, No. 11 (2001).

Sharma, B. R. 'To Legalize Physician-Assisted Suicide or Not? – a Dilemma'. *Journal of Clinical Forensic Medicine* Vol. 10 (2003): 185–90.

Shaw, A. B. 'Two Challenges to the Double Effect Doctrine: Euthanasia and Abortion'. *Journal of Medical Ethics* Vol. 28 (2002).

Sheldon, T. 'Being "Tired of Life" Is Not Grounds for Euthanasia'. *British Medical Journal* Vol. 326 (2003).

— 'Dutch GP Cleared after Helping to End Man's "Hopeless Existence"'. *British Medical Journal* Vol. 321, No. 11 (November 2000).

Silviera, M. J., A. Di Piero, M. S. Gerrity and C. Feudtner. 'Patients' Knowledge of Options at the End of Life'. *JAMA* Vol. 284, No. 19 (2000).

Singer, P. *Rethinking Life and Death*. Melbourne: Text, 1994.

— 'Voluntary Euthanasia: A Utilitarian Perspective'. *Bioethics* Vol. 17, Nos. 5–6 (2001): 526.

Sklansky, M. 'Neonatal Euthanasia: Moral Considerations and Criminal Liability'. *Journal of Medical Ethics* Vol. 27, No. 1 (2001).

Somerville, M. *Death Talk*. Montreal: McGill-Queens University Press, 2001.

Steinberg, M. A., C. M. Cartwright, M. J. Clark, J. Nathan, R. Hoffenberg, S. M. MacDonald and G. Williams. *Perspectives of Directors of Nursing of Nursing Homes on End-of-Life Decision-Making.* University of Queensland, 1996.

Steinberg, M. A., C. M. Cartwright, T. Nayman, S. M. MacDonald and G. Williams. *Healthy Ageing, Healthy Dying: Community and Health Professional Perspective on End-of-Life Decision-Making.* University of Queensland, 1996.

Steinberg, M. A., M. H. Parker, C. M. Cartwright, F. J. MacDonald, C. B. Del Mar, G. M. Williams and R. Hoffenberg. *End-of-Life Decision-Making: Perspectives of General Practitioners and Patients.* University of Queensland, 1996.

Street, K., R. Ashcroft, J. Henderson and A. V. Campbell. 'The Decision Making Process Regarding the Withdrawal or Withholding of Potential Life-Saving Treatments in a Children's Hospital'. *Journal of Medical Ethics* Vol. 26, No. 5 (2000).

Swarte, N. B. and A. P. M. Heintz. 'Guidelines for an Acceptable Euthanasia Procedure'. *Best Practice and Research Clinical Anaesthesiology* Vol. 15, No. 20 (2001): 313–21.

ten Have, H. 'Euthanasia: Moral Paradoxes'. *Palliative Medicine* (2001).

Tulloch, G. 'Avoiding the Slippery Slope in Ethics and Bioethics'. *Nursing Inquiry* Vol. 3 (1996).

— *Mill and Sexual Equality.* Brighton: Harvester Wheatsheaf, 1989.

— 'Skinner and Seeing Red'. Unpublished MA, University of Melbourne, 1980.

van Delden, J. J. 'Slippery Slopes in Flat Countries – a Response'. *Journal of Medical Ethics* Vol. 25 (1999): 22–4.

van Holsteyn, J. and M. Trappenburg. 'Citizens' Opinions on New Form of Euthanasia: A Report from the Netherlands'. *Patient Education and Counselling* (1998).

van Kolfschooten, F. 'Dutch Television Report Stirs up Euthanasia Controversy'. *The Lancet* Vol. 361 (2003).

Wade, D. T. 'Ethical Issues in Diagnosis and Management of Patients in the Permanent Vegetative State'. *British Medical Journal* Vol. 322, No. 7282 (2001).

Warnock, M. 'I Made a Bad Law – We Should Help the Ill to Die'. *Sunday Times*, December 2003.

Watson, R. 'First Belgian to Use New Euthansia Law Provokes Storm of Protest'. *Belgian Medical Journal* Vol. 325 (2002).

Wright, W. 'Historical Analogies, Slippery Slopes and the Question of Euthanasia'. *Journal of Law, Medicine and Ethics* Vol. 28, No. 2 (2000): 176.

Zinn, C. 'Police Seize Computer Files of Euthanasia Campaigner in Cancer Case'. *British Medical Journal* Vol. 3757, No. 7360 (2002).

Further Reading

Allen Jr, Norman R. 'Peter Singer: The Intrepid Ethicist'. *Free Inquiry* Vol. 20, No. 4 (2000).

Allen Jr, Norman R. 'Controversial Conceptions of Humanism'. *Free Inquiry* Vol. 23, No. 3 (2003).

Almond, Brenda. *The Philosophical Quest*. Harmondsworth: Penguin, 1988.

— *Introducing Applied Ethics*. Oxford: Blackwell, 1995.

— *Exploring Ethics*. Oxford: Blackwell, 1998.

Alvarez, Allen Andrew A. 'How Rational Should Bioethics Be? The Value of Empirical Approaches'. *Bioethics* Vol. 15, Nos. 5/6 (2001).

Amarasekara, Kumar and Mirko Bagaric. 'The Vacuousness of Rights in the Euthanasia Debate'. *International Journal of Human Rights* Vol. 6, No. 1 (2002).

Angie, A. and G. Sturgess, eds. *Legal Visions of the 21st Century*. Dordrecht: Kluwer Law International, 1998.

Batlle, Juan Carlos. 'Legal Status of Physician-Assisted Suicide'. *Journal of American Medical Association* Vol. 289, No. 17 (2003).

Beauchamp, T. L. and Le Roy Walters. *Contemporary Issues in Bioethics*. California: Wadsworth, 1989.

Benatar, Solomon R. 'Bioethics: Power and Injustice'. *Bioethics* Vol. 17, Nos. 5/6 (2003).

— 'Drop in Euthanasia Cases may be Result of Under-reporting'. *Medical Post* Vol. 39, No. 20 (2003): 61.

Blank, K., J. Robison, H. Prigerson and H. I. Schwartz. 'Instability of Attitudes about Euthanasia and Physician-Assisted Suicide in Depressed Older Hospitalized Patients'. *General Hospital Psychiatry* Vol. 23 (2001).

— 'In the Michigan Court of Appeals: People v. Jack Kevorkian'. *Issues in Law and Medicine* Vol. 18, No. 1 (2002).

Braun, K., V. M. Tanji and R. Heck. 'Support for Physician-Assisted Suicide: Exploring the Impact of Ethnicity and Attitudes toward Planning for Death'. *The Gerontologist* Vol. 41, No. 1 (2001).

Broughton, S. and S. Palmieri. 'Gendered Contributions to Parliamentary Debates: The Case of Euthanasia'. *Australian Journal of Political Science* Vol. 34, No. 1 (1999): 29.

Callahan, D. 'Defending the Sanctity of Life'. *Society* Vol. 38, No. 5 (2001).

Campbell, A. V. 'The Enigma of Death'. In *An Easeful Death*, edited by J. Morgan. Sydney: Federation Press, 1996.

Caton, H. 'Equity Goals and Quality of Life Issues'. Paper presented at the Ethics and Resource Allocation in Health Care, St Vincent's Bioethics Centre, Melbourne, 1991.

Center for Bioethics, University of Minnesota. 'On the Determination of Death'.

— 'Withholding or Withdrawing Artificial Nutrition and Hydration'.

— 'Termination of Treatment of Adults'.

— 'Resuscitation Decisions'.

Charlesworth, M. *Life, Death, Genes and Ethics*. Melbourne: ABC Books, 1989.

Christiansen, S. B. and P. Sandoe. 'Bioethics: Limits to the Interference with Life'. *Animal Reproduction in Science* Vols. 60/61 (2000).

Cimino, J. E. 'A Clinician's Understanding of Ethics in Palliative Care: An American Perspective'. *Critical Review in Oncology/Hematology* Vol. 46 (2003).

Clarfield, A. M. 'History of the Right to Die'. *Medical Post* (2003).

Clarke, G. and M. Stainsby. *Ethics and Resource Allocation in Health Care*. Melbourne: St Vincent's Bioethics Centre, 1991.

Clinton, M. and S. Nelson. *Mental Health Nursing*. Sydney: Prentice Hall, 1995.

Cohen-Almagor, R. 'An Outsider's View of Dutch Euthanasia Policy and Practice'. *Issues in Law and Medicine* Vol. 17, No. 1 (2001).

— 'Non-Voluntary and Involuntary Euthanasia in the Netherlands: Dutch Perspectives'. *Issues in Law and Medicine* Vol. 18, No. 3 (2003).

Conrad, P. 'Off Target'. *Society* Vol. 38, No. 5 (2001).

Cowley, C. 'The Conjoined Twins and the Limits of Rationality in Applied Ethics'. *Bioethics* Vol. 17, No. 1 (2003).

Coxon, A. 'Euthanasia and Physician-Assisted Suicide: For and Against'. *Ethics and Medicine* Vol. 17, No. 2 (2001).

Craig, D. A. 'Governing Ethics through Analysis and Commentary: A Case Study'. *Journal of Mass Media Ethics* Vol. 17, No. 1 (2002).

Daniel, C. 'Killing with Kindness'. *New Statesman* (1997).

Davershot, M. and H. van der Wal. 'The Position of Nurses in the New Dutch Euthanasia Bill'. *Ethics and Medicine* Vol. 17, No. 2 (2001).

De Cesare, M. A. 'Public Attitudes towards Euthanasia and Suicide for Terminally Ill Persons 1977 and 1996'. *Social Biology* Vol. 47 (2000).

De Haan, J. 'The Ethics of Euthanasia: Advocates' Perspectives'. *Bioethics* Vol. 16 (2002).

Dettweiler, U. and P. Simon. 'Points to Consider for Ethics Committees in Human Gene Therapy Trials'. *Bioethics* Vol. 15, No. 5/6 (November 2001).

Dorozynski, A. 'Highest French Court Awards Compensation for "Being Born"'. *British Medical Journal* Vol. 323, No. 7306 (2001).

Dupuis, H. M. 'Euthanasia in the Netherlands: 25 Years of Experience'. *Legal Medicine* Vol. 5 (2003).

Dwyer, J. 'Teaching Global Bioethics'. *Bioethics* Vol. 17, No. 5/6 (November 2003).

Edwards, R. B. and G. C. Graber, eds. *Bioethics*. Orlando: Harcourt Brace Jovanovich, 1988.

Emanuel, E. J. 'Euthanasia and Physician-Assisted Suicide: A Review of the Empirical Data from the United States'. *Arch. Intrn Med* Vol. 162 (2002): 142.

Flynn, T. 'The Final Freedom'. *Free Inquiry* Vol. 23, No. 2 (2003).

Foot, P. 'Euthanasia'. *Philosophy and Public Affairs* Vol. 6 (1977).

Fukuyama, F. *Our Posthuman Future*. London: Profile, 2000.

Galbraith, K. M. and K. S. Dobson. 'The Role of the Psychologist in Determining Competence for Assisted Suicide/Euthanasia in the Terminally Ill'. *Canadian Psychology* Vol. 41, No. 3 (2000).

Gallagher, R. 'Using a Trade-Show Format to Educate the Public about Death and Survey Public Knowledge Needs about Issues Surrounding Death and Dying'. *Journal of Pain and Symptom Management* Vol. 21, No. 1 (2001).

Gillett, G. 'Reasoning in Bioethics'. *Bioethics* Vol. 17, No. 3 (2003).

Glover, J. *Causing Death and Saving Lives*. Harmondsworth: Penguin, 1977.

Goodin, R. E. *Utilitarianism as a Public Philosophy*. Cambridge: Cambridge University Press, 1995.

Guinn, D. 'Honour the Patient's Wishes'. *Ethics in Cardiothoracic Surgery* Vol. 74 (2002).

Haimes, E. 'What Can the Social Sciences Contribute to the Study of Ethics? Theoretical, Empirical and Substantive Considerations'. *Bioethics* Vol. 16 (2002).

— 'Assisted Suicide, Euthanasia and the Right to End-of-Life Care'. *Crisis* Vol. 23, No. 1 (2003): 40–1.

Hentoff, N. 'Challenging Singer'. *Free Inquiry* Vol. 22, No. 1 (2001/2).

Hermsen, M. A. and H. ten Have. 'Euthanasia in Palliative Care Journals'. *Journal of Pain and Symptom Management* Vol. 23, No. 6 (2002).

Honderich, Ted, ed. *The Oxford Companion to Philosophy*. Oxford: Oxford University Press, 1995.

Humphry, Derek. 'Swiss Assisted Suicide Breaking Out'. *ERGO!* www.finalexit.org/swissframe.html.

Humphry, Derek. *Final Exit*. Harmondsworth: Penguin, 1992.

Illich, Ivan. *Limits to Medicine: Medical Nemesis*. Harmondsworth: Penguin, 1977.

Jochemsen, H. 'Update: The Legalization of Euthanasia in the Netherlands'. *Ethics and Medicine* Vol. 17, No. 1 (2001).

Jochemson, H. and J. Keown. 'Voluntary Euthanasia under Control? Further Empirical Evidence from the Netherlands'. *Journal of Medical Ethics* Vol. 25, No. 1 (1999).

Kaasa, A. 'Euthanasia and Physician-Assisted Suicide in Scandinavia'. *Palliative Medicine* Vol. 16, No. 1 (2002).

Kaplan, K. J. 'Suicide, Physician-Assisted Suicide and Euthanasia in Men v. Women around the World'. *Ethics and Medicine* Vol. 18, No. 1 (2003).

Kaufmann, W., ed. *Existentialism*. New York: World Publishing Co., 1972.

Kissane, D. W. 'The Challenge of Informed Consent'. *Journal of Pain and Symptom Management* Vol. 19, No. 6 (2000).

Kuhse, H. 'Euthanasia'. In *A Companion to Ethics*, edited by P. Singer. Oxford: Blackwell, 1993, p. 294.

Kuhse, H. and P. Singer. 'Doctors' Practices and Attitudes Regarding Voluntary Euthanasia'. *The Medical Journal of Australia* Vol. 148 (1988): 623.

La Follette, H., ed. *Ethics in Practice*. Oxford: Blackwell, 1997.

Lamb, D. *Down the Slippery Slope*. London: Croom Helm, 1988.

Lavery, J. V., J. Boyle, B. M. Dickens, H. Maclean and P. A. Singer. 'Origins of the Desire for Euthanasia and Assisted Suicide in People with HIV1 or AIDS: A Qualitative Study'. *The Lancet* Vol. 358, No. 9279 (2001).

Macdonald, W. L. 'Situational Factors and Attitudes towards Voluntary Euthanasia'. *Social Science Medicine* Vol. 46, No. 1 (2002).

Macklin, R. 'Bioethics and Public Policy in the Next Millennium'. *Bioethics* Vol. 15 (2001).

Mappes, T. A., and J. S. Zembaty, eds. *Biomedical Ethics*. New York: McGraw-Hill, 1991.

Masson, J. D. 'Non-Professional Perceptions of "Good Death": A Study of the Views of Hospice Care Patients and Relatives of Deceased Hospice Care Patients'. *Mortality* Vol. 7, No. 2 (2002).

McCall Smith, A. 'The Separating of Conjoined Twins'. *BMJ* Vol. 321 (2000).

McKneally, M. 'Witnessing Death as Lifesaving Treatment is Withheld'. *Ethics in Cardiothoracic Surgery* Vol. 74 (2002).

McPherson, G. W. and D. Sobsey. 'Rehabilitation: Disability Ethics v. Peter Singer'. *Arch Physical Medical Rehabilitation* Vol. 84 (2003).

Michels, K. B. and K. J. Rothman. 'Update on Unethical Use of Placebos in Randomised Trials'. *Bioethics* Vol. 17, No. 3 (2003).

More, T. *Utopia*. London: Dent, 1994.

Musgrave, C. F. and I. Soudry. 'An Exploratory Study of Nurse-Midwives' Attitudes towards Active Euthanasia and Abortion'. *International Journal of Nursing Studies* Vol. 37 (2000): 505–12.

— 'Ethical Issues Raised by Allocation of Transplant Resources', *International Journal of Nursing Suene* (1997).

Paris, J. J. and A. C. Elias-Jones. '"Do We Murder to Save Jodie?" an Ethical Analysis of the Separation of the Manchester Conjoined Twins'. *Postgraduate Medical Journal* Vol. 77, No. 911 (2001).

Perry, L. 'A Groovy Kind of Brain'. *The Australian*, 21 April 2004: 25.

— 'Resuscitation Decisions for Hospitalised Patients'. Biomedical Ethics. Edited by T. Mappes and J. Zembaty. New York: McGraw-Hill, 1983, p. 341.

Purchase, I. F. H. 'Ethical Issues for Bioscientists in the New Millennium'. *Toxicology Letters* Vol. 127 (2002).

Quill, T. 'Death and Dignity: A Case of Individualised Decision'. *New England Journal of Medicine* Vol. 324 (1991): 691–4.

Quindlen, A. 'In a Peaceful Frame of Mind'. *Newsweek* Vol. 139, No. 5 (2002).

Rachels, J. *The End of Life – Euthanasia and Morality*. Oxford: Oxford University Press, 1986.

Ravenscroft, A. J. and M. D. D. Bell. ' "End of Life" Decision-Making within Intensive Care'. *Journal of Medical Ethics* Vol. 26, No. 6 (2000).

Reed-Purvis, J. 'From "Mercy Death" to Genocide'. *History Review*, No. 45 (2003).

Reiter-Theil, S. 'The Ethics of End-of-Life Decisions in the Elderly: Deliberation from the Ecope Study'. *Best Practice and Research Clinical Anaesthesiology* Vol. 17, No. 2 (2003): 273–87.

Richardson, A. 'Death with Dignity: The Ultimate Human Right?' *Humanist* Vol. 62, No. 4 (2002).

— ' "Existential" Suffering not a Justification for Euthanasia'. *British Medical Journal* Vol. 323 (2001).

— ' "Terminal Sedation" Different from Euthanasia, Dutch Ministers Agree'. *British Medical Journal* Vol. 327, No. 7413 (2003).

Singer, P. *A Companion to Ethics*. Oxford: Blackwell, 1993.

— 'The Freest Nation in the World?' *New Inquiry* Vol. 20, No. 3 (2000).

— 'Changing Ethics in Life and Death Decision Making'. *Society* Vol. 38, No. 5 (2001).

— 'Freedom and the Right to Die'. *Free Inquiry* Vol. 22, No. 2 (2002).

— 'The Ethics of Belief.' *Free Inquiry* Vol. 23, No. 2 (2003).

Smith, W. J. 'Deathbed Disputation: A Response to Peter Singer'. *Canadian Medical Association Journal* (2002).

— 'Why Secular Humanism about Assisted Suicide is Wrong'. *Free Inquiry*, No. 2 Spring (2003).

— 'The Case against Euthanasia and Physician-Assisted Suicide'. *Free Inquiry* Vol. 23, No. 2 (2003).

Steel, K. 'To Kill or not to Kill'. *The Report* Vol. 29, No. 16 (2002).

Steering Committee on Bioethics (CDBI). 'Compilation of Replies from Council of Europe Member States to the Questionnaire on National Legislation Concerning Medico-Legal Autopsy Procedures'. Strasbourg: Council of Europe.

Stephens, R. L. 'The Moral Meaning of Morphine Drips: A Modern Shibboleth Denied'. *Midwest Quarterly* Vol. 43, No. 3 (2002): 346.

Szasz, T. 'The "Medical Ethics" of Peter Singer'. *Society* Vol. 38, No. 5 (2001).

Talan, J. 'Judge Denies Request to Feed Patient, 92'. *Newsday*, 4 March 2003.

Taylor, K. 'Was Dr Kevorkian Right?' *Free Inquiry* Vol. 23, No. 2 (2003).

Teays, W. and L. Purdy. *Bioethics, Justice and Health Care*. California: Wadsworth, 2001.

Tulloch, G. 'Why Euthanasia? A Reflective Response'. *Nursing Inquiry* Vol. 2 (1995).

van der Heide, A., L. Deliens, K. Faisst and T. Nilstun. 'End-of-Life Decision-Making in 6 European Countries: Descriptive Study'. *The Lancet* Vol. 361 (2003).

Vermaat, J. A. E. 'Euthanasia in the Third Reich: Lessons for Today?' *Ethics and Medicine* Vol. 18, No. 1 (2002).

Weber, W. 'Belgian Euthanasia Proposal Meets Euthanasia'. *The Lancet* Vol. 358 (2001).

Weissman, D. E., B. Ambuel, A. J. Norton, R. Wang-Cheng and D. Schiedemayer. 'A Survey of Competencies and Concerns in End-of-Life Care for Physician Trainees'. *Journal of Pain and Symptom Management* Vol. 15, No. 3 (1998).

Weitz, D. C. 'The Need for Fictive Lines'. *Society* Vol. 38, No. 5 (2001).

Wikler, D., ed. *The Definition of Death and Persistent Vegetative State*. Edited by T. Mappes and J. Zembaty, 1991.

Wilson, K. G., J. F. Scott, I. D. Graham, J. F. Kozak, S. Chater, R. A. Viola, B. J. de Faye, L. A. Weaver and D. Curran. 'Attitudes of Terminally Ill Patients Towards Euthanasia and Physician-Assisted Suicide'. *Archives of Internal Medicine* Vol. 160, No. 16 (2000).

Wolf, S., ed. *Feminism and Bioethics*. Oxford: Oxford University Press, 1996.

Wright, W. 'Historical Analogies, Slippery Slopes and the Question of Euthanasia'. *Journal of Law, Medicine and Ethics* Vol. 28, No. 2 (2000): 176.

Zucker, A. 'Law and Ethics'. *Death Studies* Vol. 25 (2001): 381–4.

Index

Active/Passive Euthanasia, 33–4, 100, 103, 137

Acts/Omissions, 26, 28–9, 55, 81, 86, 137

Adams, Dr John Bodkin, 31, 80–1, 83, 92

Adkins, Janet, 74–5

Alkmaar case (Mrs B), 98, 106

Amarasekara, Kumar, 79

America, 10, 17, 51–77, 80, 83, 96, 109, 115, 118, 134, 139

Andrews, Kevin, 124, 126–7

Ashcroft, John, 66–7

Australia, 17, 37, 89, 95, 102, 109, 114–31, 134, 139–40

Autonomy, 34–5, 38, 45, 54–5, 61, 71–2, 74, 76–7, 79, 88, 96–7, 101, 105, 117, 137, 141

Baby Doe, 15

Baby M, 15

Baby Valentina, 18

Barnard, Dr Christian, 8–9

Belgium, 95, 101–3, 122

Bentham, Jeremy, 58, 131

Bland, Tony, 19–21, 23, 32, 81–8, 90, 117, 139

Brain, 7, 9–13, 15–21, 32, 35, 38, 61–2, 77, 82, 116, 119, 122

Brongersma, Edward, 59, 104

Campbell, Robert, 85–8

Campo, Laura, 17–18

Chabot, Bourdewijn, 103–4

Charlesworth, Max, 28, 40, 45

Choice, 3–21, 23–46, 51, 54–5, 57, 67, 77, 80, 96, 115, 129, 135–7, 139, 141

Cox, Dr Nigel, 81–2, 85–8, 90

Crick, Nancy, 89, 129–30, 139

Cruzan, Nancy, 24, 26, 51, 55–6, 60, 62–3, 69, 75, 83

Death, 3–21, 23–46, 51–77, 80–93, 96–109, 114–15, 117, 119, 121–32, 136–8, 140–1

Dent, Bob, 125–7

Descartes, Rene, 70, 96

Dworkin, Ronald, 35, 52, 69, 73–5, 79, 140

England, 80–93, 96, 101, 109, 115, 118, 134, 139

Euthanasia, 21–2, 36, 41, 46–7, 61, 77, 83, 87, 88–93, 95–111, 114–31, 134, 136–41

Happiness, 75–6, 136

Hill, Chris, 118

Hippocratic Oath, 31–3

Hobbes, Thomas, 58–9, 61

Human Nature, 5, 32, 44, 76, 136

Hus, Cornelius, 118

Intentionality, 29, 31

Johnstone, Megan Jane, 47, 176

Kant, Immanuel, 59
Kass, Leon, 58, 60–1, 69, 78, 79
Kevorkian, Dr Jack, 63–4, 66, 74, 78,
    93, 127
Killing/Letting Die, 26–8, 30, 32, 35,
    46, 58, 69, 70, 81, 137, 138
Koestler, Arthur, 62
Kuhse, Helga, 27, 101, 103, 119–20,
    122–4, 132

Liberty, 41–5, 54–9, 61–2, 71, 75–7
Linares, Rudy, 16
Locke, John, 58–60
Lorber, Dr John, 14, 25

MacDonald, Wayne, 118
McEwan, John, 115–16, 118
Marshall, Trisha, 11, 32
Maslow, Abraham, 58
Mill, John Stuart, 36, 41–6, 58–9, 67–8,
    75–6, 87, 100, 105, 131, 136,
    138–9
Morrell, Mrs, 31, 80, 93
Mrs Boyes, 81, 85, 88, 90
Mrs N, 115–16

Netherlands, The, 54, 59, 65, 95–111,
    118, 122–4, 134, 138, 139–40
Nitschke, Dr Philip, 125–7, 129, 130
Nolan, Shirley, 131
Northern Territory, 95, 114, 124–9,
    132–3, 139–40
Nussbaum, Martha, 58

Oedipus, 29
Organ Transplant, 10, 39

Paternalism, 70, 72
Perron, Marshall, 124
Ploch, Marian, 11, 32

Pollack, Frances, 88
Postma, Dr Geertruida, 97–8
Pretty, Diane, 89–94, 139

QALY approach, 39–40, 139
Quill, Dr Timothy, 52, 60–5, 69, 78
Quinlan, Karen, 7, 23–6, 51, 61–3,
    69, 75

Resource Allocation, 37, 40
Rowland, Robyn, 32

Sartre, Jean-Paul, 134, 136
Schiavo, Terry, 68, 139
Shipman, Dr Harold, 92–4
Singer, Peter, 8, 10–12, 17, 19–20, 28,
    83, 100–1, 105, 123, 131
Slippery Slope, 32, 35–6, 53–4, 66, 69,
    72, 77, 89, 92, 102, 104, 137, 140
Socrates, 62
Somerville, Margaret, 25, 35, 61, 69,
    74, 106
Spears, Steve J., 119
Sperry, Dr Roger, 13
Sutorius, Dr Philip, 104
Syme, Dr Rodney, 117, 120–4, 131

Truog, Robert, 18

Utilitarianism, 96, 131, 136

Victoria, 17, 19, 24, 115–16, 121,
    124, 129
Voluntary/Involuntary Euthanasia, 30,
    33–6, 46, 61, 87, 89, 90, 92–3,
    95–6, 98–9, 101– 7, 111, 118–21,
    123, 126, 129, 138–40

Warnock, Baroness, 90–2, 94
Williams, Bernard, 87